GARDENING
IN
SMALL SPACES

GARDENING
IN
SMALL SPACES

ANGELA KIRBY

PAVILION

Also by Angela Kirby
BLOOMING INGENIOUS: THE IMPOVERISHED GARDENER'S GUIDE

JACKET PHOTOGRAPHS:
front: A goldfish pond in a tiny garden (DESIGNER Angela Kirby);
back: Wall fountain in Mr and Mrs Robert Chandler's courtyard
(DESIGNERS Matthew West and Nigel Manton).

page one: Underplanted by thriving hostas and foxgloves, the white lace-caps of the
climbing hydrangea, *H. anomola petiolaris,* brighten a wall in a shaded corner.
(Mrs Trevor-Jones, Preen Manor)

frontispiece: The skilful use of form, texture and colour transform this long, narrow
garden, hiding the boundaries and creating a sense of depth and movement.
(DESIGNER David Ffrench)

This edition first published in Great Britain in 1997 by
PAVILION BOOKS LIMITED
26 Upper Ground, London SE1 9PD

Text copyright © Angela Kirby 1997
Photographs copyright © as in the Acknowledgments on page 160
Illustrations by Nicky Cooney
Design by Grahame Dudley Associates

A CIP catalogue record for this book is available from the British Library

ISBN 1 85793 596 9

Printed and bound in the United Kingdom by Jarrold Book Printing, Norfolk

2 4 6 8 10 9 7 5 3 1

This book may be ordered by post direct from the publisher. Please contact the
Marketing Department. But try your bookshop first.

CONTENTS

INTRODUCTION

THE SMALL GARDEN — a charming phrase, conjuring up those country cottages whose plots overflow so gloriously at midsummer, as well as countless well-ordered, formal little gardens found in towns and villages about the world. No less delightful are the narrow, death-defying strips of flowers, vines and climbing roses which seem to spring directly out of the concrete to enliven many a roadside house which has nothing much else by way of a garden.

Courtyard gardens have a special magic of their own, perhaps because of their ancient lineage. They descend from the Roman *atrium*, the paradise gardens of Islam and the *patios* of southern Spain, the inner courts of castles and monasteries, down to those secret and intimate corners that are glimpsed tantalizingly through arches and open doorways around the world.

Town dwellers have always gardened in the most unpromising conditions, not least the closeness of neighbours and the shadows cast by nearby trees and buildings. Undeterred, they work away on strips of earth, gloomy basements, barren yards, narrow passages, wind-raked roofs, flimsy balconies and narrow flights of steps. There is something moving about these places, in the brave abandon of the flowers and the peace of so many small and green tranquillities.

In the country and by the sea, things may seem a little easier, but gardening there often brings other problems, not least the depredations of passing cattle or the havoc wrought by salt-laden winds. Whatever the obstacles and wherever it may be, a tiny garden may be no less intriguing in its own way than one of greater size; indeed, it will have the universal fascination of all things miniature.

Some demand an innovative, invigorating approach, others the merest tweak to enhance their existing charms. One design sets off to perfection the lean lines of a contemporary building or the classical proportions of a period house, while another redeems something altogether less distinguished. There may be good soil and a sunny, well-drained site to play with or just some damp, neglected patch in a gloomy corner, but in either case the restrictions faced in any small garden can at first seem daunting. Yet while it takes some imagination and determination to turn a handful of frequently flat square yards into a thing of beauty, it is worth remembering that despite all the difficulties, time and money spent here will have a disproportionate effect.

Ideally, a small garden has somewhere sheltered to sit which can be used as soon as the rain stops. It is safe and largely private, with areas of sun and shade protected from the worst of the winds. Many tender plants are happy there, enjoying the warm support of walls, the sharp drainage of raised beds and cool root-runs beneath the paving, while others thrive in containers of all kinds. There will be the usual problems found in any garden – and a few extra ones for good measure – but once the garden is established it should need relatively little aftercare, an important consideration for many of us. On the other hand, those who have time to spare will find it easy enough to fritter away many happy hours.

The plans in this book are not fully fledged designs for individual gardens (for each site requires its own solutions and every owner has his or her personal style), but mere suggestions for some frequently encountered situations. Zones are given where they are known; but because conditions can vary so widely within a given region and because small gardens, especially those in urban areas, are often warmer and more sheltered than others, the climate zones given in the plant lists should be regarded as merely the roughest of guides. It is always worth trying plants that are on the borderlines of hardiness in your region.

A small garden may be as simple or elaborate as its owner wishes, while the costs of construction and planting can vary enormously. These will be considerable if stone paving and antique statues are demanded, with the addition of rare or mature plants in outsize pots of hand-thrown terracotta. For something simpler, yet possibly no less effective, the outlay may be very low indeed.

Those of us who must settle for something less than the ideal may still derive a great deal of pleasure from gardening in planters, pots and containers of all kinds and wherever a little space may be found: on balconies, ledges, parapets, windowsills, steps, porches and so on. We may even, if truly desperate, garden busily and happily enough in nothing more than a hanging basket or two.

Our small gardens are intimate, often hidden treasuries; every inch of them cries out to be nurtured and embellished in some way. As that great plantswoman Gertrude Jekyll said, 'The size of a garden has very little to do with its merit. It is merely an accident, relating to the circumstances of its owner. It is the size of his heart and brain and goodwill that will make his garden either delightful or dull, as the case may be, and either leave it at the monotonous dead level, or raise it, in whatever degree he may, towards that of a work of fine art.'

— 1 —

A GARDEN TO CONTRIVE

Planning

The decision as to whether the garden is a place into which you go from the house or is an open air part of the house has a considerable effect on the design of a garden. It shifts the centre of balance, for in the first instance, there is a line of demarcation between the house and garden, in the second the whole of the living room and the garden is one unit.

SYLVIA CROWE

OPPOSITE: *A well-handled change of levels. The steps, paving details, clipped evergreens and ebulliently planted containers all contribute to its success.* (DESIGNER Christopher Masson)

OTH APPROACHES HAVE THEIR MERITS and the final decision must always be a personal one, but I prefer the line between the two to be defined, the garden to be a separate space, framed by the windows or seen through an open doorway. I love the sensation of coming out of the cool house into the bright sun, the sudden buzz of heat and scent. Then the garden remains somewhere fabulous, in the true sense, so that there is always a *frisson* upon entering it.

This magical 'otherness' of a garden can easily be ruined by a lack of surprise, by the over-use of patio doors and picture windows in unsuitable situations. In unkind climates especially, who wants to be enveloped by the rain-lashed landscape for months on end? A.D.B. Wood, in his excellent book *Terrace and Courtyard Gardens for Modern Homes,* puts it well: 'When house and landscape are locked in hermaphrodite conjunction, we lose the delight in contrast which exists more strongly when indoors and outdoors are allowed to retain their separate characters, when the relationship between the two is conducted in good-humoured tension, a sort of Mirabell-Millament alliance, in that brief, debatable land of transition.'

Where there is a sensational view – of water, the sea, or mountains, perhaps – it is tempting to incorporate it by the use of very large windows or sliding glass doors; where the weather is usually fine throughout the year, the effect is not without dramatic appeal. Some striking houses have been designed in this way and the great garden-landscapers have set them admirably in grounds of equal distinction. While admiring these, in a small garden I prefer to come upon things by stealth, catching a glimpse here, an unexpected vista there. The smaller the garden, the greater the need for such subtlety.

There will always be those who cannot be doing with planning and design, preferring to work everything out as they go along, positioning one thing here and a group of something else there,

then standing back to observe the results before shifting it all around again until the garden is to their liking. Most of us do a bit of this from time to time and many good small gardens have been made in such a way, but success is more likely if some planning is done first.

'After all, what is a garden for?' asked Gertrude Jekyll, and answered: 'It is for "delight", for "sweet solace", for "the purest of all human pleasure; the greatest refreshment of the spirits of men"; it is to promote "jucunditie of minde"; it is to "call home over-wearied spirits". So say the old writers, and we cannot amend their words, which will stand as long as there are gardens on earth and people to love them.'

We may ask the same question, and others too: not just what the garden is for, but how, in the main, it is to be used, and by whom? Is it to be merely a view? An 'outside room' where house and garden blend almost imperceptibly, perhaps with a conservatory linking the two? Or will it be valued chiefly as a stress-free hideaway, Diderot's 'sanctuary of a green and placid pleasure'?

Perhaps it must be a family garden, with swings, climbing frame, sandpit, paddling pool and barbecue; or maybe a specialist's garden, displaying collections of roses, cranesbills, alpines, rhododendrons and so on. Probably it will be a combination of some of these.

The more books consulted and gardening magazines read, the more photographs and plans studied, and gardens visited, the wider becomes the range of choices available to us. There are few better ways to spend a winter evening than to sit by the fire, planning for future glories, while on a good day, how exhilarating it is to visit some famous garden, with notebook and camera, in search of inspiration. Even the largest, grandest places may have interesting details or intimate corners which can be adapted, or planting schemes that, scaled down a touch, can be transferred to our own borders and containers. Particularly useful are those gardens divided up into small outdoor rooms, many of which might be satisfactorily reinterpreted for our own plans.

For the tyro, such foraging can reveal undreamed-of possibilities, yet even the knowledgeable are likely to find something new. Beginners benefit from the advice and example of experts, while these in turn may be jolted out of their complacency from time to time or have their prejudices challenged by those not yet burdened with a surfeit of received wisdom. An untutored eye can bring freshness and originality to a garden: with the recklessness of ignorance, rules are broken, plants grown where they should not survive and in colours that ought not to work. The result may be disaster, but sometimes it is a triumph.

I remember an innovative, erotic garden displayed at a famous flower show some years ago by a team of young designers. It did not appeal to everyone, but is the only garden of that year to remain fresh in my mind. It was so full of new ideas and the unorthodox reworking of old ones, of brave, witty touches, and sheer inventiveness coupled with youthful impudence, that I laughed out loud and felt immensely cheerful for the rest of the day.

Other virtually unknown but stimulating and informative gardens are worth visiting; those whose owners deal with similar conditions to our own are particularly useful, showing what can be done or, just as usefully, what should not be done. For unless we are masochists with unlimited time and money, it is better to garden with the soil and climate rather than to struggle against them; the

Against a backdrop of green foliage, sunlight picks out this pensive statue, the acid yellow heads of the euphorbia and a clump of pale iris in the foreground. (DESIGNER Olivia Clarke)

use of local materials and of plants that flourish in the conditions available is practical, economical and, as often as not, aesthetically pleasing.

That is not to say there should be no innovations or experiments: Sir Frederick Stern, who made a great garden in a chalk quarry, advised that, given three identical plants, one should be placed where we wish, another where the experts insist, and the third where friends advise; all, he wrote, would have an equal chance of success. Some changes and experiments there must be from time to time, for without them our gardens become predictable and reduced to a mere assemblage of horticultural clichés. Yet beware of fashion, for like time, it moves swiftly on, leaving us with its detritus.

Nevertheless, because a small garden can be accepted easily as a thing of artifice, more risks can be taken there than we might dare elsewhere. Murals, mirrors, *trompe l'oeil*, painted flower pots, artificial grass and elaborate *treillage*, perhaps absurd or pretentious elsewhere, may all be used here.

Inspiration may be drawn from other countries. The beautiful and remarkable Japanese gardens are best left in Japan, I think, but some elements of their style can be borrowed when a disciplined control of the available space, and the considered use of stones, boulders, gravel and plants of strong character, would seem eminently desirable.

Similarly, while insensitive reproductions of Spanish patios can appear brash or depressing in cooler climates, some ideas may yet be taken from Mediterranean or South American gardens: the use of white and colour-washed walls, terracotta tiles, oil-jars, grape-vines and so on, can look perfectly natural in, for instance, a sunny yard.

Yet above all, I think, a truly successful garden, however small, will, like the house, seem to evolve naturally from its surroundings, giving the impression that the garden came first, then the house arrived, found everything to its liking and settled down, in the manner of those wayward hens of my childhood that escaped their runs to ensconce themselves, fatly happy, among the contorted roots of the hawthorn trees, looking entirely at home there.

It may seem difficult to decide on a particular style or design, for, as when faced with a large, beguiling menu, the choice appears overwhelming. Yet after a while one begins to narrow things down. Are we drawn to a restrained design based on formal, geometrical lines, or to another of rugged materials, strong shapes and abstract sculpture? Might we, on the other hand, prefer to relax in something more romantic, all overblown roses, hidden arbours and pouting cupids?

Climate, personal taste and temperament, the architecture of the house and the surrounding buildings, the size, aspect and soil of the site, and not least, the amount of time and money that we are willing to lay out on design, construction and maintenance, all these help us to decide. For however passionately we garden and no matter how small our plot, many of us have limited time and money. Even when there is plenty of both, things may be different later: the enthusiasm there, but money and vigour somewhat diminished.

Careful planning and gradual changes ensure that when both the garden and its owners reach maturity, minimum maintenance is needed. Raised beds make for easy care, lawns give way to gravel or paving, plants are settled and need little further nurture. Ground cover replaces much, if not all, of the herbaceous planting, while the seasonal changes of spring bulbs, annuals and so on are confined to a few easily tended containers, reducing weeding to the occasional tweak. Yet there is no truly maintenance-free garden (and what a bore it would be) – merely one that needs less care than another. There will always be something in the way of watering, feeding and general tidying to be done; even concrete, artificial grass and plastic plants in plastic pots require a wash or a scrub from time to time.

Pleasure deferred may indeed lead to spiritual growth, but when one longs to be out in the garden, time spent on research and planning seems deeply frustrating. Yet with a little patience it can be as enjoyable as it is necessary. At first the imagination is set free and the mind allowed to flit from one idea to another like an enthusiastic but fastidious butterfly: the sensible decisions come later.

We are rewarded by the avoidance of expensive or time-consuming mistakes and in all probability the garden is more or less to our liking from the start. Some mistakes and failures there will be, for few of us are entirely sure which ideas will prove triumphant and which embarrassing disasters, but that is the fascination of it all, for as that great gardening guru Christopher Lloyd so rightly remarks, 'the ferret leads an exciting life, even if there cannot be a rabbit at the end of every passage'.

In any garden, new or old, even the smallest, it is important to absorb the atmosphere, to work with the *genius loci*, that unique spirit of the place – for each has its own. One cries out for drama and excitement, another for a quiet, even a sombre approach. Mood is affected by the architecture of the house and its relationship with the site, by near-by buildings and the surrounding landscape, not least by the sympathetic use of materials and the choice of plants. Smaller gardens need a discipline, often a degree of formality, imposed upon them, yet this can be enhanced or softened by the design and any subsequent planting.

Style, the organization of space, of proportion and scale, light and shade, the use of complementary or contrasting colours, shapes and textures, all the general principles of design apply to a small garden as they do to larger one, but appear magnified by the scale.

What is small? Like beauty, size is in the eye of the beholder; while 'garden' still conjures up images of wide lawns, gracious paths and undulating flower borders, in many countries seventy per cent or more of the population live in urban areas where most of the gardens are, in anyone's terms, small or positively tiny.

Sadly, many of these remain much as the builders and developers left them, with flimsy fencing, a few yards of concrete outside the door or, at best, a rectangle of unhappy grass cowering between mean little borders of hungry soil. Even in older properties, gardens were often laid out in this way, with the addition, perhaps, of a small, tile-edged path running round three sides of the garden, between the borders and the lawn.

Yet there does not have to be a lawn. Mrs Earle, in *Pot-Pourri from a Surrey Garden*, spoke firmly: 'In all small gardens, my advice is to avoid turf, and especially in London. It never looks well and is expensive and troublesome to maintain ... have as wide a border all round the wall as you can afford, and some red gravel or a bricked or tiled square in the middle of the garden to sit on.' One could still make a pleasant enough garden on these lines almost anywhere, and not just in London, although I am not sure about the red gravel: somehow it sounds rather ominous.

Lack of storage space for a mower makes grass impracticable for many. Furthermore, a lawn seldom does well in shade, nor will it stand up to much concentrated use in a small area: here something more hard-wearing may be chosen. Although it is commonly assumed that children need a lawn, this is not necessarily so: they are as likely to enjoy a paved area (preferably one with a paddling pool and a sandpit), where balls may be bounced and wheels can trundle freely. As Thomas Church, the distinguished American landscape architect, observed, 'Children love to go around and around, whether it's on a merry-go-round or in their own backyard. Perhaps it has something to do with the feeling of speed, or the excitement of the race and the chase, or just returning again and again to the familiar. One thing is certain: a circular route in a garden can provide more amusement hours for small children than any number of swings or slides.'

Children also adore stones and gravel, water of every kind, weeping trees, clumps of bamboo, densely planted corners and secret hiding places, all infinitely more engaging than a mangy stretch of grass. As for older children who need somewhere to hit or kick a ball about, they would be better off in the nearest park, leaving our gardens and windows unscathed.

Many gardeners do, nevertheless, want a lawn, but then there are more interesting shapes than a rectangle. Simple changes improve things: rounding one end into a horseshoe helps, as does taking a bite out of the near end or a square out of each corner. We may divide a lawn by four paths, add a paved circle at the centre and another of raised bricks or stones at its core, supporting, say, a statue or an urn. Alternatively, we may cut the lawn along its length by a narrow path leading to a bench at the far end, or reshape it into two brick-edged circles, the far one overlapping the near and raised a few inches by the depth of the brick edging.

A conservatory has to be considered at an early stage. It makes a pleasant transition from

The sturdy table and chairs look perfectly at home on a simply tiled terraced area in this well-designed small garden. (DESIGNER Lisette Pleasance)

house to garden, but takes a disproportionate amount of space, so one must weigh the advantages and disadvantages carefully.

All in all, a new garden is as awesome and thrilling as a new child; exciting to conceive, needing courage to bring forth and demanding loving care to bring it to maturity. Perhaps that is why many people who take for granted their ability to decorate houses, arrange flowers and put together clothes and accessories fall to pieces when designing a garden. Since much the same skills are needed and the same principles employed, there seems little reason why these cannot be as easily applied outside. Nevertheless, it is better not to be too ambitious at first, but to remember that, as Russell Page noted, 'the pleasures of the *tour de force* ... are apt to be transitory'.

One way to develop a garden 'eye' is to take photographs of an admired garden and then cover up some element (tree, archway, ornament and so on) and note what part it played in the composition and the effect its removal has, for better or worse, on the whole. Using tracing paper and a felt-tip pen, try similar additions and deletions on sketches and photographs of your own garden. Or place tracing paper over a photograph, then outline the garden's components, so that trees, shrubs, buildings and other major items in the scene are reduced to abstract shapes. A wall or hedge becomes a couple of parallel lines, a conifer a cone, the house a combination of squares, rectangles and triangles, and so on. This highlights the underlying design, or lack of one, and aids in the analysis of the garden; it may also help us to draw in perspective at a later stage.

It is best to tackle things logically, beginning with the boundaries: of what are they to be made, and how high? Will they give security, sufficient shelter from the winds and enough privacy? In a small garden, such questions are of paramount importance. Any internal walls, hedges, pergolas and trellis come next, partitioning the garden. Then the surfaces, another important element in a small garden, where paving is likely to take up a comparatively large amount, if not all, of the available ground. What should be laid where? How big the area needed for a table and some chairs? Is stone affordable? Will brickwork become slippery in the shade? Would gravel be a sensible solution because it is cheap, looks well and can be replaced at a later date if plans are altered? Will a change of levels make things more interesting?

Next come the main planting areas, along with the garden buildings, major ornamental elements, permanent furniture, and any water. Last of all, the planting details, containers and smaller decorative things.

Three lists are helpful:
   a. Essential improvements and additions
   b. Non-essential (but nevertheless desirable) improvements and additions
   c. What the garden has already – good, bad or merely tolerable.

Note the times when the garden will get most use. If, for instance, everyone is out all day, a seat in the evening sun is ideal; when holidays are taken at the same times each year, it is foolish to choose plants that will be at their loveliest then.

The first list might include an outside water-supply, lighting, essential paths; at least one dry, level space for a table and chairs; a few scented plants; provision for privacy, for shade in a sun-filled garden and for a sheltering screen in a windswept one. Where there is room, allow for parking, an area (preferably hidden) for clothes line, garden shed, compost heap, vegetable plot, etc. The second list might include water features, garden buildings such as a summer-house or toolshed, and other structures like arbours, arches or trellis obelisks – as well as ornaments of all kinds and any rare or spectacular plants you particularly want to grow.

To each item on the lists add the choices they suggest:

Boundaries

walls *(stone? bricks? stucco?)*

fences *(closeboard? post and rail? slatted timber? picket? trellis?)*

railings *(what style?)*

hedges *(evergreen or deciduous? clipped or informal?)*

Terraces and paths

bricks *(old or new? what colour? pattern – straight courses, herringbone or basket-weave?)*

flagstones *(genuine or reconstituted? local or imported? regular or random?)*

granite setts? gravel, cobblestones, pebbles?

tiles *(terracotta? marble? chequered?)*

concrete *(smooth or textured?)*

VARIEGATED LEAVES

TREES AND TREE-LIKE SHRUBS
Abutilon megapotamicum
  'Variegatum' Z8
Acer negundo 'Elegans' Z2
A.n. 'Variegatum'
A.n. 'Flamingo'
Aralia elata 'Aureovariegata' and
  A.e. 'Variegata' Z4
Azara microphylla 'Variegata' Z8
Cornus alternifolia 'Argentea' Z3
Ligustrum lucidum 'Excelsum
  Superbum'
L.l. 'Tricolor'
L.ovalifolium 'Argenteum' Z5
L.sinense 'Variegatum' Z7
Rhamnus alaternus
  'Argenteovariegata' Z7
Sambucus nigra
  'Aureomarginata'
  and s.n 'Marginata' Z5

SHRUBS
Acer palmatum, several cvs, inc.
  'Butterfly' and 'Versicolor' Z5
A.j. 'Crotonifolia' Z7

A.j. 'Gold Dust'
A.j. 'Golden Spangles'
A.j. 'Picturata'
Buddleja davidii 'Harlequin' Z6
Buxus sempervirens
  'Argenteovariegata' Z7 and
  B.s. 'Elegantissima'
Cornus alba cvs. inc.
  'Elegantissima' Z3
C.a. 'Spaethii' and 'Variegata'
Eleagnus many, to Z6
Euonymus fortunei, several, inc.
  'Silver Queen' Z5
Euonymus japonicus, several,
  inc.'Président Gauthier' Z7
Fuchsia magellanica var. gracilis
  'Variegata' Z6
Hebe x andersonii 'Variegata' Z9
Pachysandra terminalis 'Variegata'
  Z5
Pieris japonica 'Variegata' Z6
Pittosporum, many, inc. P. tobira
  'Variegatum' Z9
Viburnum tinus 'Bewley's
  Variegated' and 'Variegatum' Z7

Vinca major cvs. inc. 'Variegata' Z7
V. minor cvs. Z4
Weigela 'Florida Variegata' Z5
Yucca aloifolia 'Variegata' Z8
  Y. filamentosa 'Bright
    Edge' Z4 and Y.f. 'Variegata
  Y. gloriosa 'Tricolor and Y.g.
    'Variegata' Z7
  Y. recurvifolia 'Variegata' Z8

CLIMBERS
Coronilla glauca 'Variegata' Z9
Hedera, many, to Z5
Jasminum officinale
  'Argenteovariegatum' Z7
Lonicera japonica
  'Aureoreticulata' Z4

PERENNIALS
Acorus calamus 'Variegatus' Z3
Arum italicum cvs. Z6
Astrantia major 'Sunningdale
  Variegated' Z6
Brunnera macrophylla 'Dawson's
  White' Z3

Hosta (many)
Iris foetidissima 'Variegata'
I.pallida. 'Argentea Variegata '
I.p. 'Variegata'
Phlox paniculata 'Harlequin' and
  'Nora Leigh' Z4
Phormium (many) Z8
Polemonium caeruleum 'Brise
  d'Anjou' Z2
P. 'Variegatum' Z6
Pulmonaria, many, to Z3
Sisyrinchium striatum 'Aunt May'
  Z8
Symphytum grandiflorum
  'Hidcote Variegated' Z5
S. x uplandicum 'Variegatum' Z5

timber *(decking? railway sleepers or cross-ties? boards? slabs?)*
mixtures of any of these? – and so on.

Water
a pool *(what shape? raised or flush? what about the children?)*
moving water *(wall-fountain? bubble-fountain? canal, cascade?)*
containers *(cisterns, troughs, shallow bowls, birdbaths?)*
irrigation system?

Garden buildings and other structures
summer-house? pavilion? gazebo? toolshed? bowers and arbours? grotto? arch? tunnel? trellis dividers? obelisks?

Ornaments
columns, pediments, pedestals, chimneypots?
mirrors, murals? *(trompe l'oeil, illusion trellis?)*
vases *(urns, oil-jars, forcing-pots?)*
sculpture *(classical? contemporary? abstract?)*
found objects (*boulders, driftwood, ancient artefacts?*)

As these key items will play a significant part in the scheme, it is a good idea to position them on the plan at the start.

The third list itemizes the pluses and minuses of the existing site, what must go or stay, how assets may be emphasized and disadvantages transformed. Take the large, blank wall often found in town gardens. It may seem intimidating, but a wall, no matter what its aspect, gives useful privacy, shelter and support for climbing plants – an important advantage when growing-space is limited. With walls of stucco, decent brickwork or local stone, we are in luck, but even the raw look of new bricks and concrete can be tamed with a few coats of paint. By painting just the bottom section of the wall, to about eight feet (2.5m), say, the eye is drawn from the reaches above down into the garden, to settle more happily there. Trellis panels add to the effect, while a pavilion, bench or wall-fountain anchors the eye even more firmly within comfortable range.

Lack of privacy or an ugly view provides an excuse to run decorative trellis along the top of walls and fences or to make a generous planting of mature trees and shrubs. Though not necessarily the cheapest of solutions, either of these could be the making of the garden and should prove worth the outlay. Close-meshed trellis panels disguise down-pipes, air-ducts, dustbins (trash cans) and other necessities while adding interesting vertical accents to the design – and support for more plants that can climb.

Where the only garden is at the front of the house, privacy is a major consideration if it is to be used for entertainment and relaxation. How this is achieved will depend on the size of the garden and the style of the property: in some areas there are restrictions on changes to the façade or on the height of walls and fences. Small trees and shrubs are usually allowed, but should not overhang the roadway outside at a height hazardous to passers-by, nor interfere with high vehicles, overhead lines and cables. Where appropriate, a tallish wall or fence, perhaps topped by trellis, gives the necessary seclusion and some protection from noise and pollution. If neither walls nor fences are possible, plants do the job almost as well; one or two small trees, some tough, bushy shrubs or clumps of bamboo, all give a good deal of protection. Within such an enclosure, we may enjoy the garden as we please, while a small arbour or pergola will shield us from the high windows of neighbouring properties. If none of these remedies is available – for reasons of size, style or possible prohibitions – the front plot will be for display only, but can still be a delightful form of gardening which gives much pleasure to owners, neighbours and those who pass by.

Much should be made of any advantages the garden has. Where there is a view worth having, this dominates the plan to an extent. It is enhanced if framed in some way – by a pair of plants or a group at each side, a gateway between handsome piers – or if half-seen between near-by buildings, in the way one catches a tantalizing glimpse of silver between the hotchpotch houses of an old fishing village. Even in towns and cities a view may be of near-by water or distant hills, but it is more likely to be of church spires, an interesting gaggle of rooftops, or even something as arresting as mill-chimneys and water-towers.

Another more intimate kind of view, such as a flamboyant tree or interesting architectural detail, may be borrowed from the surroundings: by rearranging a few plants or by installing, say, a moon-window in a wall, hedge or trellis, we kidnap the view for ourselves.

Also prized are good garden buildings, walls, steps, unusual plants and gnarled trees with furrowed bark or twisted branches. Some of these things may be moved about and regrouped (quite large plants can be moved, by specialists if necessary), while others are left where they are but accentuated in some way, perhaps by the treatment of the surrounding ground surfaces, or by selective pruning and complementary planting.

Dame Sylvia Crowe, in *Garden Design*, wrote: 'The need of each owner should be developed into a garden individual to himself, and in the sincerity which such a garden expresses, it is likely to give pleasure to others.' One should not be intimidated when taking over a garden, no matter how

---

PLANTS FOR BUTTERFLIES AND MOTHS

Ageratum	Echium	pink and purple)	Sedum spectabile
Armeria maritima	Eryngium	Lunaria	Solidago
Aster (Michaelmas daisies)	Erysimum	Nepeta	Tagetes patula (single, e.g.
Aubrieta	Escallonia	Pelargonium (scarlet)	'Naughty Marietta')
Brachyglottis 'Sunshine'	Hebe	Petunia (single)	Leucanthemum x superbum and
Buddleja	Hedera (adult forms)	Phlox	cvs.
Caryopteris x clandonensis	Heliotrope	Primula (single)	and most other species with
Ceanothus	Hesperis matronalis	Reseda odorata	flowers of the single daisy type.
Centranthus	Iberis	Rubus	A clump of nettles and a path of
Choisya	Lavandula	Syringa (esp. purple and mauve)	rough grass will also be
Dianthus barbatus	Lobularia maritima (white,	Scabious	appreciated

well-established or treasured by the previous owners. If things are not to our liking, we can change them; a garden that is not a true reflection of our own needs and desires becomes a soulless thing, however beautiful. Courage and a degree of ruthlessness are needed.

Nevertheless, think hard before removing mature trees and shrubs. Not only is this an expensive and often disruptive procedure, but they can add character to a garden in a way that is difficult to replace. They may seem nothing special at first, but often respond well to a judicious trimming. The removal or thinning out of the lower leaves and any twiggy growth can reveal well-shaped trunks and branches. Privet, magnolia, lilac, euonymus and ceanothus are some plants successfully treated in this way. Others, mainly evergreens, can often be clipped into some kind of topiary shape.

Some trees may have to go if they are diseased, take too much light, damage walls and foundations, or are just plain horrid, but their removal can also cause structural damage. In many areas, trees are subject to protection orders and their unauthorized removal incurs substantial fines. A tree-surgeon will advise, check with the necessary authorities and carry out any permitted work. If a healthy and otherwise handsome tree casts too much shade, thinning of the crown introduces light and air while preserving the shape of the tree and the shelter and privacy it provides. It is astonishing how this improves a gloomy, overcrowded garden – it seems to sigh with relief, like someone casting off their stays.

For the rest, try to wait before making any changes: a year is not too long. This gives us time to note, as the seasons pass, any hot-spots, frost-pockets, waterlogging, wind-tunnels (very common among tall buildings) and areas of light or shade at different times of day.

In all but the tiniest spots, it pays to make inspections throughout the year, checking first from one angle and then from another. Must one or several plants be removed in this place to open things up a bit, or should some be planted in another to provide privacy or to give shelter? How about a small pavilion here or a large specimen plant there?

The house will have its own contribution to make, in its shape and detail and as a backdrop for the plants: are changes or embellishments desirable? A conservatory, French windows, some shutters? If period features have been removed, both house and garden will be given back their proper dignity when these are restored. On the other hand, if the house has strong, clean lines, it would be as well to remove any irrelevant bits and pieces, fiddly little flower beds or insignificant statuary from the garden, replacing them with plants of bold outline or striking foliage, swathes of ground cover, abstract sculpture or large found objects such as boulders, driftwood or industrial relicts.

Winter is the best time to walk round the garden or to look on it from within for this kind of assessment; free from the camouflage of leaves and the distraction of flowers, strengths and weakness

A magic carpet of cyclamen and crocus beneath the bare and lichened branches of an interestingly shaped old tree. (Mrs Merton, Burghfield Manor)

OPPOSITE: *White ivy-leaved pelargoniums froth out of a Cretan pot, which is set in a gravel circle at the centre of a brick path in Mrs Dymock's small, pretty Berkshire garden.*
(DESIGNER
Lucy Huntington)

in the underlying design become clear. Sit for a while at an open doorway or upstairs window, considering the garden and what lies beyond: is there a vista to be discovered or a monstrosity to be blocked out? For many weeks the small garden will be experienced more as a view than as occupied space; happily, it will be handsome in its way, at all seasons; in winter especially, it will benefit from a strong design and a framework of evergreens. The worse the weather and the surroundings, the more we need some charming thing just outside the windows to cheer and console us, distracting our gaze from any infelicities beyond.

While eyesores or an entrancing view may be unveiled only at leaf-fall, the discovery of unsuspected treasures happens at all seasons. Beverley Nichols, a once-popular English author, is now rather neglected, but it was his descriptions of the making of his gardens, of the trials and errors endured in the process, that made me realize there was more to gardening than my father's 'all hands to the weeding' approach. In *Down the Garden Path,* Nichols describes such an inspection of the garden: 'When I arrive in my garden, I make The Tour ... I step from the front window, turn to the right and make an infinitely detailed examination of every foot of ground, every shrub and tree, walking always over an appointed course. There are certain very definite rules when you are Making The Tour. The chief rule is that you must never take anything out of its order. You may long to see if a crocus has come out ... but it is strictly forbidden to look before you have inspected all the various beds, shrubs and trees.'

Gardens – town gardens in particular – should be restful places. If the garden matches or is sympathetic to the scale, style and period of the house and neighbouring buildings, if the materials used are chosen to blend in with those of the architecture, this goes a long way towards producing a sense of unity. Simplicity of design and an absence of undue fussiness in the detail are also helpful in this respect.

Restraint in the variety of materials used and in at least the background planting will be rewarded; we must learn to jettison some of our darlings. When space is limited, most of us suffer from a strong temptation to cram in one of each of as many different plants as possible, but this is seldom a successful approach; fewer types of plants, in groups of three, five, seven or more of that same plant, are more soothing.

Here is no real sacrifice; against a background of evergreen and deciduous plants chosen from those with green, yellow, silver, purple, reddish-bronze, blue and variegated foliage, we may add a few dramatic specimens, flowering shrubs and herbaceous perennials, together with seasonal bulbs and annuals for drama and exuberance. This is best not overdone, for too much excitement in a confined space can lead to a feeling of unease. Such rules may be ignored, of course, and with panache, but should be borne in mind, even while deciding to override them.

While some sites and conditions are easier to work with than others, things may change over the years, or even overnight. Certain factors are beyond our control: buildings are suddenly thrown up near by and others demolished, winter gales will mutilate one lovely tree or uproot another that has previously given us years of privacy. Worse, we come home to find a neighbour's hedge towering over us and a new highway at the bottom of the garden – challenging but not insuperable problems;

as Mrs Earle snapped, 'If gardening were easy, even under favourable circumstances, we should none of us care to do it.'

Recalcitrant neighbours are often the trickiest of problems; *cultivate your neighbours* should be engraved on every gardener's heart. The good and tolerant are more vital to the success of our small gardens than any amount of well-rotted manure, while Mr and Mrs Indignant Next-Door will do their damnedest to thwart every plan.

Who plans the enchanted garden, who directs
The vista best, and best conducts the stream.

JOHN ARMSTRONG (1709–99)

OPPOSITE: *A gilded sphere gleams against the sober tiles and brickwork of this interesting wall fountain, which is framed and softened by the surrounding plants.* (DESIGNER David Ffrench)

~ 2 ~

THE WELL-DISPOSED GROUND

Design

Let not each beauty ev'ry where be spied,
Where half the skill is decently to hide.
He gains all points who pleasingly confounds,
Surprizes, varies, and conceals the bounds.
Consult the genius of the place in all.

ALEXANDER POPE (1688–1744)

ONCE THE GARDEN STYLE IS DECIDED UPON, drawing up a design concentrates the mind quite wonderfully. Even when dealing with a small plot, or thinking of minor changes and improvements to a bigger one, some sketches and a simple plan will be useful, but for anything larger or for an empty site, a more detailed approach is worthwhile.

A drawing-board is ideal but a cork notice-board makes a reasonable substitute. A long measuring tape, a flexible metal rule, tracing and graph paper, masking tape, scissors, pencils, pens, an eraser, ruler, compass and a set-square (those from a school geometry set will do) are needed, while some stiffish coloured paper, a French curve (for drawing curving shapes) and a template for circles have their uses; all are available from stationers and art suppliers.

A plan of the site may be included with the house deeds and this can be blown up to a workable size, but check the measurements, for they are not always accurate. If an architect was involved in the construction or renovation of the house, his plans may show at least the outline of the plot.

Failing these, make a rough sketch plan. Then take measurements of the garden with the long tape, from end to end, side to side and diagonally; mark these on the sketch plan, and double-check them. From this draw an accurate plan on graph paper, using as large a scale as possible. Mark in the house, boundaries and other permanent features, including drain runs and manholes as well as all large plants, for this helps to keep the facts in mind. Mark tree-trunks with a dot or circle and use a dotted line for the spread of the canopy, as this may affect the position of pools, seating areas and any underplanting. Show areas of shade from trees, buildings, etc., by light cross-hatching. If the garden is larger or a complicated shape, make a separate scale plan for each section.

As said before, boundaries are of great importance in a small garden, so note their condition: are the fence-posts rotten, the walls crumbling, the trellis broken? Are hedges gap-toothed or dying?

OPPOSITE: *The limited space in this small front garden has been used to great effect. Gravel, brickwork, clipped evergreens, a small statue and effective planting all play their part. (Mrs P. Sinclair, Lime Tree Cottage)*

OPPOSITE TOP: *An imposing pot of* Erysimum *'Bowles' Mauve', under-planted with viola and saxifrage, at the centre of a path of old stable tiles crisply edged by clipped hedges. (Peter Aldington, Turn End)*

Add the condition of other trees and shrubs, some of which may be diseased, rotten or dead. Paths and paving also: are they loose, cracked, unstable? Garden buildings: sound or derelict? (And if demolished, where can we keep the tools?) Are water features leaking, pumps working?

Mark in the position of downstairs doors and windows; these provide the main sight-lines into the garden and may affect the size and positioning of features in the design. Vertical measurements, such as the height of the boundaries, interior walls or hedges, doors, windows, etc., go in. Add north and south, for it is easy to forget how the garden lies and the resulting areas of sun, shade and prevailing wind.

Small changes of level go on the plan. If the garden is on much of a slope, the fall is measured. Place a spirit level on a long plank, one end of which rests on the top of the slope; when the plank is level, a pole or stiff rule is run down from the other end to the ground and the measurement noted. Repeat down the slope; the measurements, added up, show the fall of the land, which is noted on the plan (an extra drawing of the slope in profile is helpful here).

When all is down, leave the master-plan unchanged and use tracing paper and pencils, or photocopies, for alterations. It is easier to discard a number of tracings at this point than to rectify errors in the garden later. For a simple layout, the master-plan, the ideas marked out on the various tracings taken from it and a few rough sketches are enough.

With a slightly larger garden or when major changes are proposed, a grid-plan is very helpful. Draw squares on tracing paper to a scale based on a unit taken from the first plan, such as a recurring or dominant feature of the house, to make a design relating house to garden, well-proportioned and unified. The unit might be based on a door, window, the spaces between them, an angle of a wall or a projecting bay. Failing these, something from the garden can be used, such as the space between upright supports of fences and walls, an arch or gateway, or existing paving. Too small a unit of measurement results in a fiddly design; one too large produces something weak and unresolved.

Place the traced grid over the master-plan; these and any subsequent tracings are fixed in place by drawing-pins (thumbtacks) to a cork board or with masking tape to a drawing-board. Draw subsequent plans on tracing paper placed over the grid. A shape taken from the architecture of the house or the surroundings can suggest the mainstay of the design. If, for example, there is a semi-circular or three-sided bay window, a design based on a circle or hexagon picks up the shape; an L-shaped angle at the corner of the house suggests a terrace, lawn and planting areas reflecting that. Where the view is of tall gables or other sloping angles, the design might use diamond and triangular shapes or strong diagonal lines across the site.' ... A garden where there has been a lack of decision on the relative proportions of one thing to another has a nondescript appearance. Either the parts should fit together to make one indivisible whole or one element should dominate over all the others,' wrote Sylvia Crowe, the English landscape architect.

Having drawn a grid at 90 degrees to the house, interesting designs are made by turning it at 45 degrees across the plan (or part of it). This works well for a small garden, often producing something more interesting than the usual square or rectangular layout.

OPPOSITE BOTTOM: *A box-hedged, formal knot-garden makes a satisfying, disciplined centrepiece to the surrounding beds of more relaxed planting. (The Tudor House Garden, Southampton, Hampshire)*

When stumped for ideas, cut yourself free from preconceptions by making a tracing that shows only house and boundaries, leaving the garden a blank on which to experiment with shapes – circles, squares, rectangles, octagons, hexagons and triangles cut out from pieces of coloured paper, which can be moved about at will.

Do this without first thinking what they might represent. Combine two or three pieces of the same shape but perhaps of different sizes (all within the scale of the grid, including fractions and multiples of its squares); allow one shape to contrast with or overlap another; set a circle within a square, a diamond within a circle, or let one circle take a bite out of another, and so on. Chop and change with sizes and shapes until you have a good idea of the possibilities. In a very small garden, it is best to work with only one or two basic shapes.

Study abstract paintings and collages for further inspiration. This also works with less formal designs, made with the help of the French curve and the compass, or copied from patterns found on tiles, fabrics and oriental rugs. The influential landscape architect Sir Geoffrey Jellicoe took one of his designs, that of the rose garden at Cliveden, from Paul Klee's *The Fruit*, and this is a practice which can provide plenty of inspiration. He also advised, 'You first prepare a design in the normal way, you find it uninspiring, you place the drawing at a distance, preferably upside down, you gradually become aware that it suggests a shape that is foreign but friendly to any idea of your own.' Later he added, 'At first reading this advice might seem whimsical. It is not. It is the introduction to abstract art, that vast field of the creative subconscious.'

After playing around for a while, a pattern will evolve that pleases you. Outline this and colour in to represent various elements – green for grass, darker green for plants, blue for water, greys and brown for hard surfaces and so on. Then swap everything round, changing the lawn to gravel, a flower bed to a pool, etc., to see if that works better.

Formal designs are often best in small gardens, especially those in urban situations where, apart from their own firmly delineated shape, they are set within an angular framework provided by the strong horizontal and vertical lines of the neighbouring buildings. However, the most severe layouts can be tempered or completely disguised by plants, while a design based on circles and half-circles, the gentlest, most feminine of the geometrical shapes, gives a softer (though still formal)

GOLD AND YELLOW LEAVES

TREES AND TREE-LIKE SHRUBS
Acer shirasawanum 'Aureum' Z6
Gleditsia triacanthos 'Sunburst'
   Z3
Laurus nobilis 'Aurea' Z8
Ligustrum ovalifolium 'Aureum'
   Z5
L. tschonoskii 'Vicaryi' Z5
Sambucus canadensis 'Aurea'
   Z3
Sambucus nigra 'Aurea' Z5
S. racemosa 'Plumosa Aurea' Z4

and several conifers

SHRUBS
Berberis thunbergii 'Aurea',
Ilex crenata 'Golden Gem'
Lonicera nitida 'Baggesen's Gold'
   Z7
Philadelphus coronarius 'Aurea'
   Z5
Ribes alpinum 'Aureum' Z2
R. sanguineum 'Brocklebankii'
   Z6

Viburnum opulus 'Aureum' Z3

CLIMBERS
Hedera helix 'Buttercup' Z5
Humulus lupulus 'Aureus' Z5
Jasminum officinale 'Aureum' Z7
Lonicera japonica 'Aureoreticulata'
   Z4

PERENNIALS, HERBS AND GRASSES
Filipendula ulmaria 'Aurea' Z2
Hakonechloa macra 'Aureola' Z5

Hosta (some)
Melisa officinalis 'Aurea' Z4
Milium effusum 'Aureum' Z6
Origanum vulgare 'Aureum' Z5
Thymus x citriodorus 'Aureus' Z7
Tolmiea menziesii 'Taff's Gold'
   Z7
Valeriana phu 'Aurea'

A pair of clipped conifers

A small arbour

A design for a square garden. Gravel paths and flower beds edged by clipped box are surrounded by borders of trees, shrubs and perennials.

Thickly planted border

Paths and terrace of bricks, gravel or stone flags

The sundial can be replaced by a standard fruit tree, a tripod of bean poles or an obelisk of trellis

Formal beds, edged by clipped evergreens and planted with flowers, herbs and vegatables

York stone, ferns and chamomile frame a tiny, brick-edged pool, surrounded by low, raised beds. (RHS Chelsea, 1992)

effect. Circles must also conform to the scale of the grid and this is done by placing the spike of the compass on one of the intersections and using the length of one of the squares, or its fractions and multiples, for the radii.

Shapes alter the way a garden is perceived. A circle makes a restful shape for a seating area, is innately satisfying for a pool, and calming in a design based mainly on sharp angles. The eyes are drawn to a circle and rest contentedly there, indifferent to unsightly views beyond – a useful device.

Most of us feel more at ease within a clearly defined area which gives an illusion of safely enclosed space. Squares, too, have a settled, secure feel to them, a *je suis, j'y reste* quality; by placing two, overlapping at one corner, diagonally across the garden, the security remains but with an added sense of movement.

Rectangles are the most usual shapes for a town or village garden. Running away from the house, they draw the eye along their length to the boundary at the far end, but unless there is something of interest there to focus on (or we break up the length by splitting up the garden in some way), there is little to engage or charm us.

We may use a paved path, flower borders or pleached trees to divide the lawn and direct us

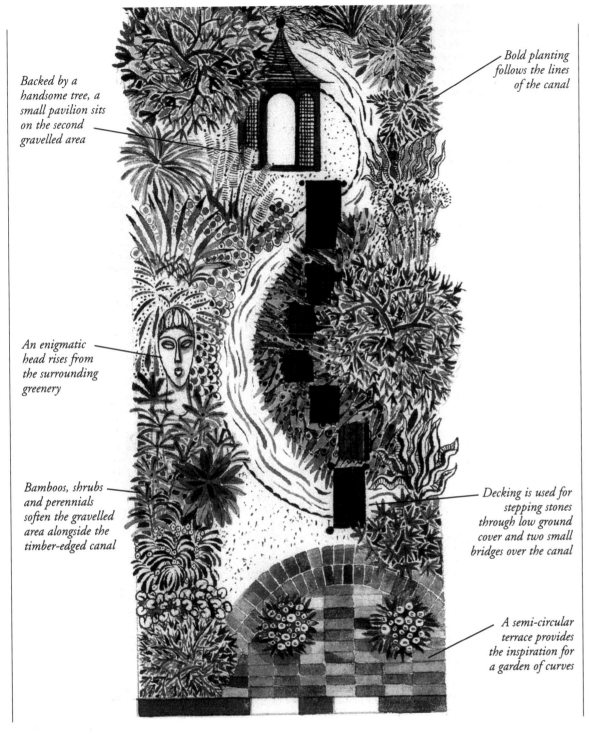

A shallow, winding canal appears to flow through this garden.

Bold planting follows the lines of the canal

Backed by a handsome tree, a small pavilion sits on the second gravelled area

An enigmatic head rises from the surrounding greenery

Bamboos, shrubs and perennials soften the gravelled area alongside the timber-edged canal

Decking is used for stepping stones through low ground cover and two small bridges over the canal

A semi-circular terrace provides the inspiration for a garden of curves

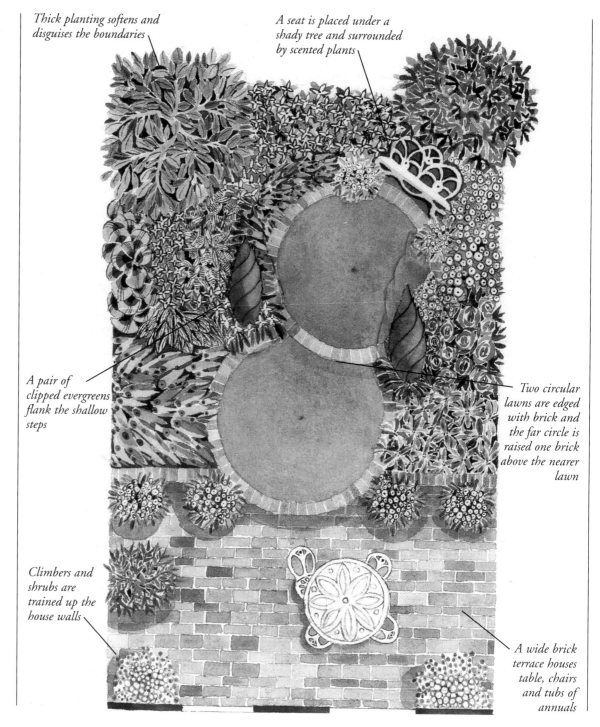

A small terrace and two overlapping, brick-edged circles of lawn or gravel, surrounded by lush planting, bring interest to a rectangular plot.

Thick planting softens and disguises the boundaries

A seat is placed under a shady tree and surrounded by scented plants

A pair of clipped evergreens flank the shallow steps

Two circular lawns are edged with brick and the far circle is raised one brick above the nearer lawn

Climbers and shrubs are trained up the house walls

A wide brick terrace houses table, chairs and tubs of annuals

towards a statue or a seat: perspective will appear to narrow the width of the path. Create a false perspective to 'lengthen' a short garden by narrowing the width of the path as it runs and using plants or ornaments that become progressively smaller towards the far boundary. Use colour in a similar way in both planting and paintwork: hot, bright colours march boldly towards us while pale, cool shades recede modestly into the distance.

Or we might step out from the house on to a terrace, climb two shallow steps up to a small area of lawn or gravel surrounded by plants, cross this and pass through an archway or rose tunnel into a paved circle with a pool. A second paved seating area like this is useful if that beside the house is shaded, and small changes of level emphasize the divisions of a garden and make it more interesting. My own garden, only sixteen feet wide by eighteen feet deep (4.5 x 5m), has a paved rectangle outside the back door, surrounded by scented plants and just large enough for a table and four chairs. One shallow step leads to a second area, also paved, with a pool at its centre; this slight difference has a disproportionate impact, clearly defining the two areas and, perversely, making the garden seem larger.

The divisions of a garden may be actual – interior walls, hedges, trellis, etc – or merely suggested, by changes of ground levels, patterns and textures, or by allowing the eye to wander round and through groups of plants that screen one part from another, inviting us to discover what lies behind. This division works even in a solidly paved garden, using groups of plants, mainly evergreens, in containers.

BOTTOM LEFT: *Russian vine billows over a doorway into this small, vividly planted garden on two levels.* (DESIGNER Jo Passmore)

BOTTOM RIGHT: *A large ammonite and pots of agapanthus stop the unwary from stumbling into the pool. Standard rose 'The Fairy' flowers generously over a long season while pots of lilies and bedding plants add scent and colour.* (DESIGNER Angela Kirby)

RED, BRONZE OR PURPLE LEAVES
(use strong colours with discretion)

TREES
Catalpa x erubescens 'Purpurea' Z5
Cercis canadensis 'Forest Pansy' Z4
Cordyline australis Purpurea Group Z10
Cotinus coggygria 'Royal Purple' and others Z5
Malus x purpurea cvs. Z4
Prunus x blireana Z5
P. cerasifera cvs., inc 'Nigra' and 'Pissardii' Z4
Sambucus nigra 'Guincho Purple' Z5 and S.n. 'Purpurea' Z5

SHRUBS
Acer palmatum (several) Z5

Berberis thunbergii atropurpurea and cvs. inc.'Atropurpurea Nana', 'Red Pillar' and 'Rose Glow' Z4
Prunus cistena 'Crimson Dwarf' Z3
Rhododendron 'Elizabeth Lockhart'
Salvia officinalis 'Purpurascens', and S.o. 'Tricolor' Z5
Weigela florida 'Foliis Purpureis' Z5

CLIMBERS
Vitis vinifera 'Purpurea' Z6

PERENNIALS
Acaena microphylla Z6
Ajuga reptans 'Atropurpurea' and A.r. 'Burgundy Glow' Z6
Cimicifuga simplex 'Elstead' and

Atropurpurea Group Z5
Heuchera 'Palace Purple' Z6
Euphorbia amygdaloides 'Purpurea' Z7
Foeniculum vulgare 'Purpureum' Z5
Lobelia cardinalis Z3
Oxalis triangularis 'Atropurpurea'
Phormium (several) Z8
Rheum palmatum 'Atrosanguineum' (and others) Z6
Tellima grandiflora 'Purpurea' Z6
Trifolium repens 'Purpurascens' Z4
Viola riviniana Purpurea Group, (Viola labradorica) Z2 plus some Sedum, Sempervivum and grasses

ANNUALS AND BIENNIALS
Amaranthus cruentus Z5
Canna, many, inc. 'Roi Humbert' Z8
Ricinus communis 'Impala' (and others) Z9
Perilla frutescens var. crispa Z8 and P.f. rubra

To increase the illusion of size in my garden, the two paved areas are surrounded by narrow but crowded borders and partly divided by thickly planted containers, grouped to make a niche for a statue on one side and a hideaway for a bench on the other. Such blurring of the boundaries, making it difficult to see where a garden begins and ends, is another way of expanding a small space. It also disguises unattractive walls and fences, often found in small gardens. Sylvia Crowe describes this sort of in-depth planting as a 'melting boundary', one, that is, designed 'to allow the eye to lose itself in shadow'.

Gardens, or parts of them, designed on the diagonal or with sharp angles have a feeling of movement and some drama about them: two or three areas of grass, paving, plants or even water marching diagonally across the plan are stimulating, inviting the eye to follow them towards some final resting place, perhaps a summer-house or comfortable bench on a raised, semicircular base.

In such ways we can make short gardens seem longer, narrow gardens wider or small gardens larger; more generous plots have a charming diversity when divided and subdivided in similar fashion.

It is best to leave the very smallest gardens (those little more than two or three yards or metres square) undivided, with the centre free of planting and clear of containers, to get the maximum use of the floor space. Use walls or fences instead as vertical planting areas or dramatize them in some other way.

Ground surfaces, an important part of any design, are particularly significant in these small gardens, being often the main decorative element. A tiny diamond-shaped lawn, brick-edged and set among thickly planted ground cover; concentric circles of bricks or granite setts; a star or sunburst of pebbles; slates or stone slabs set within a square of railway sleepers (cross-ties); all of these, surrounded by low plants or contrasting paving materials, have a strong impact in a small area.

Two topiary spirals flank the central arbour

This tiny garden has two paved areas, one higher than the other, a small lily-pool and three mirror-backed arches on the far wall to give a feeling of light and space.

Stone flags, on two levels, provde a stable base for table, chairs and bench

A raised vase is planted with graceful, shade-loving plants

Spheres of clipped evergreen, set off by strappy foliage and the glaucous leaves of a hosta, enliven a shaded path of quarry tiles in effective contrast to the sunny garden above. (DESIGNER David Ffrench)

Each shape and texture gives a slightly different effect. Space being limited, the more static designs based on circles and squares are usual, but some sense of movement is gained by the use, say of, undulating borders of tiles and mosaic or setts laid in a fishtail pattern.

Smooth stone and marble slabs are suitable for more formal schemes; decking, gravel, bricks, slate and tiles can be used formally or informally. Crazy paving (random flagstones), granite setts, cobblestones, pebbles and shells are at home in less formal gardens, as are railway sleepers (cross-ties), old boards, wooden stepping stones, wood chips and crushed bark (tanbark). Mark on the plan any ground patterns that play a major part in the design.

Those small gardens used only as a view can have a central feature, maybe a vase on a pedestal or a raised pool with a fountain. Here, too, the walls are important, planted and decorated to amuse, or mirrored to give an illusion of somewhere beyond. This sort of treatment is particularly useful in areas where access is difficult (basement areas, light-wells, etc.); these should not be wasted, especially where there is no other garden.

When a garden is surrounded by other buildings, these will have a strong, sometimes an overwhelming influence; if they are interesting, we can 'borrow' them for a view, but when too large or too near, appearing to crowd in, they are best 'pushed back' in some way. Where possible, paint them in soft, receding colours; otherwise use plants and screens that allow mere glimpses of the buildings. It is tempting to build high screening walls or fences, but they should never be higher than the width of the plot; this may seem self-evident, but I saw a garden, no more than thirteen feet wide (3.75m)

FAR LEFT: Climbing rose 'Bantry Bay' and Hedera helix *'Buttercup' enliven a grey wall and frame the wrought-iron gate. (Mr Fuller, Crossing House)*

A topiary 'punctuation mark' brings this softly planted garden into focus. (DESIGNER *Lisette Pleasance*)

where the owners had erected a towering wire fence all around and covered this with creepers in an attempt to blot out a neighbouring school. Far from being protected, we seemed crushed and isolated there, while the creepers looked sinister.

A lowish wall or fence, four or five feet (120–150cm) high, is better, topped off by some two feet (60cm) of 'honeycomb' brickwork or strong trellis. This gives seclusion but has a lighter, airier feel than solid wood or brickwork. With climbing plants (vines), some large shrubs or small trees, it makes an efficient, not too domineering screen. The force of the wind, broken by a pierced or slatted screen, creates less turbulence than when swirling over a solid wall. For extra privacy near the house, make the first few panels of trellis higher and more closely meshed.

Although this shields at ground level, perhaps the garden is overlooked from the upper windows of neighbouring buildings, while near-by horrors of any height may remain visible. Here one must effect something within the garden, to protect at least one part of it by pergola and trellis screens or by trees and groups of plants. The nearer these are to us, the more effective the screen and larger the area blocked out.

My neighbours have a garden overlooked by houses on either side. Across it, about a third of the way along, there is a simple wooden pergola, covered in summer by deciduous climbers (vines), which makes a secret dining-room. In winter, leaves fall and the house gets all available light when it is most needed.

But to return to the plan: with boundaries marked, style decided upon and the main features drawn in (walls, terraces, lawns, paths, steps, trees, planting areas, garden buildings, pools, etc.) we move on. Pergolas, arches, rose tunnels and any permanent furniture go in next, together with the larger containers and ornaments. Finally, the detailed planting plans are marked in. If it seems difficult to imagine how all this will look, blow up photographs of the existing plot and the surrounding properties. Tape tracing paper or transparent film over the photographs and draw with felt-tip pens any new buildings, hedges, ornaments, specimen plants, etc. No sketching skills are needed, just rough impressions, using squiggles or bare outlines.

A cardboard model, glued or held together by adhesive tape, is helpful. Leave one side open, where the house would be be, for a viewing point. Plants, garden furniture, ornaments, etc., painted or cut out from pictures, are mounted on thin card and moved about the set. Bits from a toy garden or landscape accessories for model railways also help to give the three-dimensional effect. I use a small marble Eros, leaning on his bow, from my mother's 1913 wedding cake, whenever I want a statue for one of my plans; oddly shaped pebbles stand in for abstract sculpture. Place the model on a table and peer through the open side: this gives a good idea of how things will look when the garden is established.

It is important to look forward, considering not just the immediate effect of every plant but their eventual height and spread, how much light they may take, the parts of the garden they may hide, the leaves they may drop in a pool, the shade they will cast and the impact all this will have on the design. How often one sees a young weeping willow planted beside a miniature pool in a small garden, and practically weeps oneself to think how it will be hacked to little more than an unsightly

Bright paint and a stained-glass window transform a humble garden shed. Topiary domes and spirals, together with the restrained planting, distinguish this simple design. (Jonathan Baillie, London)

A moss-grown urn is the deliciously sombre centre of this unusual small water-garden. (DESIGNER Malcolm Hillier)

stump, all its beauty and grace of form lost, in the attempt to keep it from enveloping everything in sight.

Water in a garden enhances and emphasizes a design, bringing it to life in a way that nothing else does quite so well. Similarly, electricity, creates endless felicities within a garden at night. Trick out the tree with strings of tiny lights like fireflies, place softly glowing lamps about the terrace and, uplight downlight and sidelight, plants and ornaments. Light will linger over leaves and flowers, show a tree's graceful silhouette, throw dramatic shadows, 'graze' over textured walls, paving and polished bark, float across the surface of water or gleam up from beneath.

The designing of front gardens brings particular problems. Here is no place for an overdose of misplaced originality. A front garden, whatever its style, should contribute to the attractions of the neighbourhood rather than compete with them in a vainglorious way.

> *Still follow every sense, of ev'ry art the soul,*
> *Parts answ'ring parts shall slide into a whole,*
> *Spontaneous beauties all round advance,*
> *Start ev'n from difficulty, strike from chance,*
> *Nature shall join you; time shall make it grow.*

ALEXANDER POPE (1688–1744)

~ 3 ~

AND HOW THE CRAFT
SHALL BE DONE

Construction

Now bricklay'rs, carpenters and joiners,
With Chinese artists and designers,
Produce their schemes of alteration,
To work this wond'rous transformation.

ROBERT LLOYD (1733–64)

OPPOSITE: *Here,*
unusually, a decorative
and roomy pavilion is
placed so as to join two
neighbouring gardens,
opening out on to both.
(DESIGNER David
Ffrench)

IT IS ALL VERY WELL TO DREAM AND TO DRAW PLANS, but the time comes when the construction of the garden must begin. An unnerving moment, for one is about to be put to the test: any mistakes will be there for the world to see, or so one imagines. In fact, nobody else is likely to care very much, so it is best to take a deep breath and get on with it all.

This is no place for a full description of the techniques of earth-moving, bricklaying, slabbing, carpentry and so on, but to understand something of them is useful, making life easier when dealing with landscapers and builders.

The smallest details of construction have a disproportionate effect in a little garden. It is deeply satisfying to do everything oneself (a great deal can be done, even by a beginner, with the help of a DIY manual) but never be tempted to fudge things. If in doubt, it is better, quicker (and, in the end, probably cheaper) to use experts. The lists and plans drawn up earlier will be helpful: if everyone working in the garden has a copy of the overall plan, as well as a detailed description of their own work in it, there should be few mistakes.

Well-recommended firms or individuals are essential; there are many fly-by-nights around. A good general builder will cope with most things in the hard-landscaping line, but seldom with laying a lawn or planting. A local garden centre may recommend a firm to take care of everything, while some have their own landscaping teams; check that someone well qualified is in charge of the gang, which may be a group of trainees and cheerful itinerants.

A specification is useful, detailing what is to be done, how, and in what order, together with the materials to be used, their type and quality, including grade of turf and approximate sizes of plants. This, together with the plans, allows little room for misunderstandings as long as it is also clear who is to do what, thus preventing tiresome demarcation disputes.

Taking photographs of both our own and neighbouring properties before work begins helps to avoid arguments about any damage done while work progresses. Not all builders own up to their misdeeds and some neighbours, alas, make fraudulent claims. Photographs should settle matters.

With everything listed, get three quotations for the work (the cheapest is not necessarily the best). These should be itemized so that if you proceed with only part of the work, those costs will be clear. Get written quotes for any changes or additions to the specification, or costs may shoot up alarmingly. Someone who has underestimated may be tempted to make it up on the extras, so make copies of all quotations and subsequent amendments.

Before work begins, make sure all necessary permissions have been obtained. These change from time to time and vary in certain localities, so do not rely on what everyone thinks: check anew.

If the only access to the garden is through the house, as it so often is with small gardens, whenever possible get all materials in and all debris out before interior decoration is started or carpets laid.

When working in an established garden and planning only minor changes, everything is simple enough: first repairs, rebuilding and repointing, applying paint, stains and wood-preservative. Then small structural changes: grass replaced by paving (or the other way round), slight changes of levels, the addition of a wall-fountain or pool, etc. After that, new structures – trellis, arbours, pergolas, etc. – are put up, next the statues, urns and so on, followed by any permanent furniture. Only then can planting begin; if attempted beforehand, some plants are sure to be damaged.

ROSES

CLIMBERS AND RAMBLERS
MEDIUM TO LARGE
Rosa banksiae 'Lutea'
'Albéric Barbier'
'Climbing Cécile Brünner'
'Félicité Perpétué'
'François Juranville'
'Gloire de Dijon'
'Madame Alfred Carrière'
'Madame Caroline Testout'
'Madame Grégoire Staechelin'
'Mermaid'
'New Dawn'

MEDIUM
'Aloha'
'Bantry Bay'
'Casino'
'Compassion'
'Dream Girl'
'Climbing Etoile de Hollande'
'Golden Showers'
'Hamburger Phoenix'
'Handel'
'Guinée'
'Leverkusen'
'Meg'
'Mrs Herbert Stevens'
'Nymphenburg'
'Parade'

'Parkdirektor Riggers'
'Phyllis Bide'
'Climbing Picture'
'Pink Perpétué'
'Climbing Pompon de Paris'
'Reine des Violettes'
'Ritter von Barmstede'
'Schoolgirl'
'Souvenir de Claudius Denoyel'
'Swan Lake'
'White Cockade'
'Zéphirine Drouhin'

SHRUB ROSES FOR SUN
'Alfred de Dalmas'
'Angelina'
'Boule de Neige'
'Cardinal Hume '
'Cécile Brünner'
'Comte de Chambord'
'Cramoisi Supérieur'
'Felicia'
'Golden Wings'
'Graham Thomas'
'Gruss an Aachen'
'Madame Pierre Oger'
'Nymphenburg'
'Perle d'Or'
'Rosa glauca'
'Vick's Caprice'

'Yesterday'

SHRUBS ROSES THAT TOLERATE A
DEGREE OF SHADE
'Ballerina'
'Blanc Double de Coubert'
'Buff Beauty'
'Cornelia'
'Fru Dagmar Hastrup'
'Lavender Lassie'
'Louise Odier'
'Madame Isaac Pereire'
'Penelope'
Rosa x odorata 'Pallida' (syn. Old
   Blush China)
Rosa primula
Rosa xanthina 'Canary Bird'
'Sarah Van Fleet'
'Schneezwerg'
'Stanwell Perpetual'

CLUSTER ROSES
'Apricot Nectar'
'Arthur Bell'
'Chinatown'
'Dainty Maid'
'Dearest'
'Dusky Maiden'
'Escapade'
'Iceberg'

'Lilac Charm'
'Magenta'
'Ma Perkins'
'Margaret Merril'
'Pink Parfait'
'Plentiful'
'Rosemary Rose'
Polyantha (excellent for v.
   small gardens)
'Mevrouw Nathalie Nypels'
'The Fairy'
'White Pet'
'Yvonne Rabier'

STANDARDS
'Albéric Barbier'
'Ballerina'
'Bonica'
'Canary Bird'
'Félicité Perpétué'
'Nozomi'
'Swany'
'The Fairy'
'White Pet'
'Yesterday'

Try also the ever-growing range of ground-cover roses, miniature and patio roses, and David Austin's New English Shrub roses.

When major work begins on an old garden there is always clearing up to be done before the plan can be laid out. Even if the site is supposedly ready, probing often reveals horrors just below the surface. Rubble, jagged metal, broken glass, perennial weeds, tree roots, etc., all must be dug up and removed. Deadly asbestos is sometimes found in the roofs and linings of old sheds: if so, contact the environmental authorities. Rubbish, rat-bitten huts, derelict trellis, crumbling rockeries and unwanted plants can go, but save ornamental ironwork, ancient bricks, paving stones, edging-tiles, bits of marble, slate, etc. for possible use later. Even half-bricks, shards of china, broken urns and interesting pebbles have possibilities, while rubble is useful for the foundations of terraces, paths, paving and walls.

Keep good topsoil left over from any excavations, stacking it in small heaps well away from any subsoil. Use it to change levels or, suitably enriched, in raised beds and the larger containers. In long-neglected gardens the soil will be in desperate need of improvement. New topsoil should be added if the existing stuff is very scant and poor. When trees have to be removed or trimmed, get specialists to do this. Neighbours may be willing to share the costs.

A new site should have been cleared and left more or less level; but again, under a thin spread of soil, there may be the builder's detritus and sometimes a thick layer of sterile subsoil left there when the foundations were excavated: this has to go, a slow, hateful job. Sometimes soil is compacted by machinery, the stacking of materials and the comings and goings on the site: if so, dig over destined planting areas, by hand or mechanical means, leaving parts that are to be paved or built upon firm and undisturbed.

Waterlogged soil is usually the result of soil compaction, broken drains or a high water-table, so one must break up compacted soil or install and repair the drains. In severe cases, raised beds might be the answer; these are excellent in a small garden, wet or not, and are easily maintained while making interesting changes of level. Where the soil is not actually stagnant but merely damp, or just on the boggy side, many charming plants will be happy there: willows, ornamental rhubarbs, primulas, water irises, ferns and a host of others.

For security reasons, the boundaries are done next, lessening the danger of tools, materials and plants disappearing overnight: in high-risk areas this is best done *before* the ground is cleared, unless that would make access for machines and materials impossible.

Walls are the best of all boundaries for a garden: strong, handsome, giving warmth and shelter while muffling noise. Local brick and stone are excellent, but rendered and painted concrete blocks are cheaper and admirable for many situations.

All walls need good foundations and if over three feet (1m) high, should be strengthened by piers every eight feet (2.5m) or so. A four-foot (1.2m) wall topped by airy trellis or honeycomb brickwork saves on bricks and labour and usually costs less than a solid wall.

Bricks are laid with staggered joints: the patterns or 'bonds' add variety to the walls; a decorative layer of roof or 'creasing' tiles is sometimes laid on top or set between the top layer of bricks and the rest. There may, however, be local restrictions on the height of garden walls in your area, so check before work starts.

As to fencing, interwoven panels or those with a wavy edge often have a flimsy, fake-rustic appearance, seldom right for a small garden. Board fences are a better choice, being strong and unobtrusive; stout, upright posts are sunk into the ground and firmed in with rubble and concrete or inserted into metal post-supports: between the posts go panels of vertical boards nailed to horizontal rails. Buy ready-made panels or, with awkward sizes and where access is difficult, assemble them on site.

Picket fences are perfect for cottage gardens and clapboard houses: their refined cousins, the spindle fences of New England, are equally charming. A tall, close-set picket or board fence makes an effective boundary for a modern house and can also be used for internal dividers, perhaps with the slats set a little wider to give a lighter feel. A simple, temporary fence is used to protect a young hedge until it grows to a reasonable height and thickness but gives some security and privacy meanwhile.

Hardwoods are painted, stained or left to weather naturally; softwoods need paint or a suitable wood preservative (not creosote, which is toxic to plants; use it for any parts that will be sunk into the ground).

In small, informal gardens, hurdles of willow, hazel, brushwood, reeds, etc. look charming. Bamboo fencing and screening is attractive, useful for camouflaging ugly boundaries and sympathetic to gravel, decking, boulders and foliage plants.

When walls and fences are up, or repaired, trellis can be added. The very best, bought or homemade, is well worth the expense, being strong, long-lasting and good-looking; cheap trellis is the worst of false economies. Fitting trellis panels to an existing wooden fence is easy. There are metal post-extenders available; the extenders are slipped down over the old posts and the new lengths are inserted. When putting up new fences, choose posts long enough to accommodate the trellis. The average builder, if not watched, nails long, conspicuous uprights on walls to support the trellis above: fortunately there are other methods. For panels no more than three feet (90cm) high (often the maximum if the effect is not to be overpowering), use shorter, more decorative posts, with ornamental finials and an ogee finish, screwed or bolted to the wall. They should be the height of the panels, plus about eighteen inches (45cm). Alternatively, screw special metal shoes to the top of the wall to hold the posts. Just as easy, cement metal pipes or rods into the top of the wall, bore matching holes in the posts and push them down over the rods. Such attention to detail makes a vast difference in a small garden and one has to be firm about it. Incidentally, plant shrubs and climbers (vines) between fence posts, not against them, to avoid disturbance if the posts are replaced at some time. If stuck with some ugly posts, hide them with something quick-growing and bushy planted alongside.

With boundaries established, we can lay out the design. Taking the measurements from the plan, mark straight lines with pegs and connect them up with white string or tape. Use a builder's square to check angles and a long spirit level to see that the ground is flat where necessary. A compass (made from two pegs tied to a piece of string the length of the radius) draws circles and curves: push one peg into the ground and scratch circles and half-circles with the other, then mark with pegs

or sand. The use of pale pegs, string, sand or shingle against dark earth shows the plan clearly and makes checking easy. Adjustments can be made at this stage: paved areas may need to be enlarged, paths widened or narrowed, a proposed building or statue moved a little to the left or right, and so on. To mark flowing curves, push and pull a length of heavy rope or flexible hose until the desired shapes are achieved: in cold weather, hot water softens a stiff hose.

With the plan established, check again, from an upstairs window if possible. There should be no hint of the 'designer garden', of being too-clever-by-half. No matter how skilfully a garden is laid out, one should never be overly aware of this; nothing kills the mood so surely. Canon Ellacombe, an English cleric and enthusiastic gardener, wrote: 'Here is another rule – to avoid everything that suggests man's artifice, or even suggests man's labours. Of course there must be artifice and there must be human labour, but they should be kept out of sight as much as possible.' There are exceptions to this, for some quirky gardens – patently things of labour and the wildest artifice – succeed, but then they have been not so much designed as evolved out of the personality of their owners.

If there are changes of level to be made, this is done next. Remember not to make any sunken areas too deep, as this gives the disquieting impression of being in a well or a fish-tank. Paving and flower beds often end up above the level of the damp-proof course or the air-bricks of an old house and must then be reinstalled well below them.

In one of my gardens, this entailed lowering the soil by about a foot (30cm); an area large enough to make a good-sized paved area was excavated and the surplus topsoil spread over the rest of the garden. This then became eighteen inches (45cm) above the paving and was retained by low brick walls, with three shallow steps leading to the lawn, thus turning necessity into virtue. Even these low retaining walls need foundations; add a row of weep-holes at two-foot (60cm) intervals just above ground level to allow surplus water to drain freely.

Necessary or not, it is easy enough to make one area a little higher or lower than the other: three to six inches (8–15cm) makes quite a difference in a small garden; raising one area just the height of a brick above another is often enough.

First, roll up any decent turf and put aside while work progresses (scruffy or unwanted turf is excellent deposited at the bottom of raised beds, planting holes and large containers). Now remove the topsoil from both areas and keep aside in small heaps on ground sheets or paved areas. Spread a few inches of subsoil from the lower area over the part to be raised, rake level, and roll or stamp down. Then return the topsoil, unless one or both of the new levels will be paved, gravelled or built upon. No matter how carefully soil is consolidated, it continues to settle for some weeks, so allow for this by leaving it a little proud.

As to the terrace, the larger, the better within the space available and the constraints of the overall design, allowing room for a table and chairs, and possibly for folding chairs or other reclining seats. A small table and four chairs need not less than eight feet by eight feet (2.5 x 2.5m). If this levelled area runs almost the width of the house and extends out by at least ten feet (3m), there should be space for dining, reclining and play.

Work out how much furniture will fit in or, alternatively, how large the terrace must be to accommodate every piece needed, by marking the pieces on the grid-plan, remembering that each piece or group needs about one yard or metre all round it to allow everyone to move around freely.

Many materials make a good terrace, either singly or in combination; these, together with the way they are laid, will contribute to the mood of the overall design. Courses running away from the house give an impression of length, those laid across the site appear to widen and shorten it, while diagonal courses give a sense of directional movement.

Bricks are laid in innumerable ways; often the simplest patterns are the best, and entail little or no cutting. Use gravel or pebbles to fill in odd corners instead of cutting bricks and stone to fit. Cobblestones are charming, laid flat-side up (on edge where you want people to keep off). In most soils, large slabs of natural stone are heavy enough to be laid directly on sand or mortar without a hardcore base, but a firm foundation is needed in soft soils and for all other materials (especially in areas subject to severe frosts). As you work, give the terrace a slight fall of about one inch in six feet (2.5cm/2m) away from the house or towards the drains.

The first job is to clear the ground of plants, roots and topsoil, to a depth that allows for a minimum of four inches (10cm) of rubble, a two-inch (5cm) layer of mortar or sand, plus the depth of whatever surface material has been chosen. The top of this final layer should be at least six inches (15cm) below the damp-proof course. Similar preparations are needed for most paths in the garden, unless on very firm ground: again a slight fall or camber will ensure that surface water does not

The colourful bedding-plants in massed containers bring luxurious warmth to this timber deck in Philadelphia. (DESIGNER Marina Kaiser)

Water from an old iron pump gushes into a brick trough filled and surrounded by the lush foliage of ferns, foxgloves, arums, ivies and primulas. (DESIGNER Roger Platt *RHS, Chelsea, 1995*)

puddle. When laying gravel or unjointed slabs, a porous membrane spread beneath suppresses weeds but allows moisture through: cut holes in the membrane for planting where necessary.

For a simple, home-made deck, prepare the ground in much the same way by clearing, levelling and firming down the soil or subsoil before adding a three-inch (8cm) layer of gravel topped by another three inches of sand. Larger, weight-bearing decks need a concrete foundation: the planks are supported by joists which rest on bricks cemented to the concrete. It is a skilled job and there may be local regulations about its construction or a building permit required: this should be checked with the local building authorities (local building commission).

Safety is easily overlooked in the thrill of creation, yet potential dangers are present even in a small garden. Water is essential for the plants and useful for cleaning walls, paving, etc., while pools, canals, cascades and even shallow bowls are a source of much pleasure. Nevertheless, young children drown in an inch or two of water, and older children trip, panic and get into difficulties in quite a shallow pool, while a loose or an unstable surface at the pool's edge is dangerous for anyone. I have fallen into my own ponds often enough to know that it is, at best, a painful and dispiriting experience which leaves one feeling remarkably foolish and does nothing for the lilies and the fish. There can still be water, perhaps in the shape of a raised pool with a broad parapet that forms a seat, but with very young children it is better to choose a self-contained wall-fountain or one where the re-circulating water falls into a shallow bowl and down through pebbles into the concealed tank below. Give an existing pool a decorative, metal grille or empty it and turn it into a sandpit until the children grow.

Electricity is useful for tools, lights, pool-pumps, barbecue spits, etc.; treat it with care and respect; a residual circuit breaker is a must, and all wires and cables must be protected against accidental damage. All fittings must be suitable for exterior use. There should be good lighting by the front and back doors, for both ease of access and security. Lighting around the perimeter and the garden approaches is an additional bonus for security, while it makes sense to light potential hazards, such as changes of level or pools. In small gardens, it is only civil to see that the lighting does not intrude upon our neighbours. When water-pipes and electric cables are needed out in the garden, lay them in ducts beneath the terrace during the construction work even if there are no definite plans to use either, for this keeps open the options for future use.

As always, a front garden needs special consideration, especially if space is needed for a car – not the most decorative of garden ornaments. Placed a little to one side and given a plant-covered screen, it will not be too obvious, but avoid parking under a tree, even one that does not drip sticky residues over the paintwork, for birds perching in the branches produce just as terrible results. Better to plant something eye-catching near by and focus attention there instead.

Security in a front garden is important. Good lighting, prickly plants, gravel and trellis go some way to deter thieves. Permanent garden furniture, favourite ornaments and expensive containers are best secured in some way - set in concrete, screwed to a fixed object or fastened with strong chains to bolts in the ground or walls. A really determined thief may still whisk everything away in the night, but light-fingered opportunists will be deterred; keep the more desirable plants out of the reach of passers-by. A fierce dog is the ultimate deterrent but does an inordinate amount of damage when rushing after his quarry and may chew the postman.

Gardens on a sloping site can be delightful and full of interest, but need careful handling to achieve their full potential. Many small gardens are approached from a basement, or lower ground floor, where the ground rises, often quite steeply, from a small paved area. This can be rather daunting, but things improve if the paved area is enlarged and the slope pushed back to make retained beds, and perhaps pools, on two or three levels. There are many plants for both sun and shade that enjoy such well-drained conditions, trailing down and softening the retaining walls. If there is a flat area at the top of the slope, or one can be made there, approach it by a central flight of steps or, where there is room, by one at each side of the terrace: a sweep of curved steps looks wonderful.

Behind one big-city house lies a small garden, far below street level. There is a paved area in front of the French window and the rest of the garden rises gently, in three curved, terraced beds, to a paved circle in a far corner which catches the midday sun. Around it, crossed by a stone slab, is a semicircular canal where fish and plants lived contentedly. The surrounding walls are covered by mirror and this in turn by well-made trellis set between handsome trellis piers. With the boundaries thickly planted and climbers (vines) sprawling across the trellised mirrors, all sense of being trapped in a gloomy well is banished.

A house on ground that slopes down and away from it needs a level platform on which to 'sit'. This may be a wooden deck, or a terrace on ground shored-up by the method known as 'cut and fill'. Earth is removed from a lower part of the slope and used to level up the area above and behind. Such a deck or terrace needs a balustrade or low parapet of some kind, if house and inhabitants are not to seem in danger of falling off the edge. Continue the cut-and-fill terracing down the garden; when the slope is gentle, retain the earth in the new, shallow levels by low walls of brick, stone, planks or sleepers (cross-ties). On a steeper slope, with serious walls higher than about thirty inches (75cm), professional help is needed, but done well, such a series of steps and terraces, each perhaps with a different mood, makes a fascinating garden.

Most plants that climb will be equally happy to sprawl and fall, unless they have very stiff stems, so rambling roses, clematis, jasmines and so on can dangle their pretty heads down the terraced walls to meet those climbing up. The boundary walls and fences on either side will have to be 'stepped' down a steep slope but will run on gently down a slight one.

Well-made steps, however few, are an important part of any design; shallow flights may be replaced by ramps for wheelchair access. In a small cottage or seaside garden, old concrete steps look charming when rendered and painted white, blue, pink and so on, with matching walls and floor; add contrasting paintwork on doors, windows, shutters and furniture. Steps are also made from bricks, stones, logs and sleepers (cross-ties).

A cascade of water running down through narrow, stepped canals or gutters on either side of the steps into pools, canals or hidden tanks below is an unusual and safe way of introducing water into the garden where children play. Although the sound of running or falling water is utterly delightful and screens out less attractive noises near by, it can be an irritant to neighbours, especially at night; then the flow should be adjusted, or turned off upon retiring.

A fortunate few small-garden owners have streams running through their plots. The rest of us can only grind our teeth and make do with artifice – the merest suggestion of a stream, or small

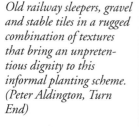

Old railway sleepers, gravel and gravel and stable tiles in a rugged combination of textures that bring an unpretentious dignity to this informal planting scheme. (Peter Aldington, Turn End)

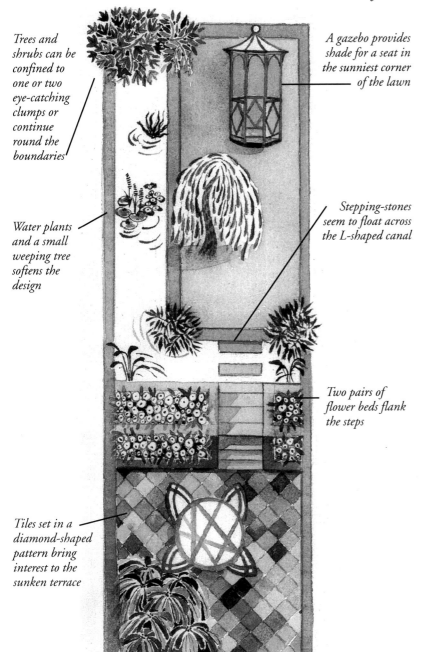

Trees and shrubs can be confined to one or two eye-catching clumps or continue round the boundaries

A gazebo provides shade for a seat in the sunniest corner of the lawn

Water plants and a small weeping tree softens the design

Stepping-stones seem to float across the L-shaped canal

Two pairs of flower beds flank the steps

Tiles set in a diamond-shaped pattern bring interest to the sunken terrace

A basement garden. Two tiers of flower beds flank the steps leading up to an L-shaped canal edging a lawn or paved area with a pavilion and a weeping tree.

WATER PLANTS FOR SMALL POOLS

VERY SMALL WATERLILIES
good for the smallest pools and container pools
Nymphaea candida
N. x *helvola* Z4
N. 'Laydekeri Lilacea'
N. 'Odorata Minor' Z3
N. 'Pygmaea Rubra' Z6
N. tetragona 'Alba' Z3

SMALL-MEDIUM WATERLILIES
Nymphaea 'Froebelii' Z5
N. 'Gonnere' Z5
N. 'Firecrest' Z5
N. 'James Brydon' (takes a little shade) Z7
N. 'Laydekeri Fulgens' Z5
N. 'Marliacea Albida' Z5
N. 'Marliacea Rosea' Z5
N. odorata Z5
N. 'Odorata Sulphurea' Z6
N. 'Rose Arey' Z7
N. 'William Falconer' Z5

OXYGENATORS
Ceratophyllum demersum (hornwort) Z8
Elodea canadensis (Canadian pond weed) Z3
Hottonia palustris (water violet) Z6
Lagarosiphon major Z8
Myriophyllum aquaticum (water milfoil) Z10
Ranunculus aquatilis (water buttercup) Z5

FLOATERS
Aponogeton distachyos (water hawthorn) Z10
Eichhornia crassipes (water hyacinth) Z10
Hydrocharis morsus-ranae (frogbit) Z4
Lemna minor (duckweed) Z4

MARGINALS
Acorus calamus (sweet flag) Z3
A.c. 'Variegatus' Z3
Acorus gramineus (Japanese rush) Z6
A.g. 'Variegatus' Z6
Calla palustris (bog arum) Z4
Caltha palustris C.p. alba and 'Flora Pleno' Z3

Carex elata 'Aurea' (Bowles' golden sedge) Z7
Juncus decipiens 'Curly Wurly' Z4
J. effusus 'Spiralis' Z4
J. inflexus 'Afro' Z4
Iris laevigata (Japanese water iris) and cvs. inc. 'Dorothy', 'Snowdrift' 'Rose Queen' 'Variegata'
Iris pseudacorus 'Variegata' Z5
Iris versicolor and I.v. 'Kelmesina' Z4
Lobelia cardinalis Z3
L. 'Dark Crusader' Z5
L. 'Russian Princess' Z5
Myosotis scorpioides (water forget-me-not) Z5
Sagittaria sagittifolia 'Flore Pleno' (arrowhead) Z7
Typha minima (dwarf reedmace) Z6
Zantedeschia aethiopica (arum lily) Z8

POOL-SIDE PLANTS FOR MOIST GROUND
Astilbe Z5
Filipendula ulmaria 'Aurea' (yellow-leaved meadowsweet) Z2
Hemerocallis (day lily) Z4
Hosta (plantain lily) Z4
Iris ensata (Japanese flag) many cvs. inc. 'Variegata' Z4
I. sibirica (white, blue and purple forms) Z4
Lobelia siphilitica (worth it for the name alone but a lovely plant) Z4
Lysimachia nummularia 'Aurea' (creeping jenny) Z4
Lythrum virgatum 'Rose Queen' (purple loosestrife) Z3
Matteuccia struthiopteris (ostrich feather fern) Z2
Mimulus (monkey flower) according to type, Z3-7
Persicaria bistorta 'Superba' Z4
Rheum 'Ace of Hearts' (ornamental rhubarb) Z6

canals and rills, which may sound rather grand but are just long, narrow and shallow pools, with straight (or just occasionally, curved) sides. A slightly wider-than-usual canal, set across the garden from side to side, crossed by a bridge or stepping stones, and appearing to flow on through a low arch at each end, divides and brings diversion to a long, narrow garden. By fitting both arches with mirrors, the illusion is strengthened, for the water appears to flow in and on out of sight. (Those who think this a little over the top can let the ends of the canal disappear between clumps of plants.) Any stepping-stones here, as elsewhere, should be stable and level, appearing to float lightly on the water.

With good-quality liners and preformed shapes, it is easy to make pools and canals. Formal shapes look best in small gardens and some manufacturers will make up liners for one-off designs; black is the best colour. Water tanks, obtainable from plumbers' merchants, make strong little pools. Whether using flexible liners or rigid, preformed shapes, excavate the ground to the required depth, removing stones and roots, then lay a two-inch (5cm) layer of sand over the bottom. Where the ground is particularly stony, line with loft-insulation or special lining supplied by pool manufacturers. Use a spirit level on a plank across the excavation to see that it is completely level all round: if not, things will never look right. A preformed liner can now be lowered into place. When using a flexible liner, drape it over the top of the hole, then place a few bricks or similar weights around the edge to keep it in place. Add water slowly, easing the liner into position without stretching, pleating it where necessary as the water pulls it down and presses it against the sides of the pool; remove the weights when it is nearly full, then trim the liner, leaving about six inches (15cm) overlap and hold this down with turf, sleepers (cross-ties), bricks or flagstones; all these (except turf) should overhang the pool by a couple of inches to hide and protect the liner.

Raised pools are made with either preformed or flexible liners, or by using any watertight and non-toxic container, supported and disguised by walls of brick, stone, slate, tiles, wood and so on, over level ground topped with sand.

The size of a liner is calculated as the width of the pool plus twice its depth, by its length plus twice the depth, allowing a few inches extra to both length and width for the overlap. A pump for a small fountain can be added (run on a low-voltage cable); in small gardens, only a gentle bubbling thing is needed, rather than tall or elaborate jets. The jet must be no higher than the distance from its nozzle to the side of the pool, or else a great deal of water will be wasted, the pond will need topping up regularly and the surroundings will be slippery.

Pools and canals can be as shallow as one pleases; most marginal plants will grow in a few inches of soil and water. Leave newly filled pools for several days before planting and two weeks before adding fish. Fish need a minimum of eighteen inches (45cm), but even then, in areas where the pool could become frozen solid, they must be taken inside during the cold months. With this depth, a shallow planting-ledge is needed round the sides for the marginal plants; cut this out during excavation. Failing this, the plants can rest in their containers on piles of bricks or blocks at the right level.

With the hard landscaping done, buildings, structures and large ornamental features installed,

prepare the lawn and planting areas; if the ground has been cleared properly, these will just need to be dug over lightly.

The preparation of planting beds is described in the next chapter, but dig over any areas designated for a lawn and rake level, removing stones and perennial weeds. Then firm down, treading it over two or three times if necessary and level again if any unevenness appears. Rake again and apply a suitable fertilizer; it is then ready to seed or turf. Turf is not that expensive and is essential where there are pets or children, for it takes light use almost at once. A brick, stone or concrete border to a lawn saves on the task of edge-trimming while emphasizing the shape.

Finally, when there are small children, a sandpit is often the best place for them: made as part of the overall design, these can be attractive and when no longer needed may be used as planting spaces or as pools.

Cela est bien dit, mais il faut cultiver notre jardin' ... and the best is yet to come.

> *With just contempt he spurns all former rules,*
> *And shows true taste is not confined to schools,*
> *He barren tracts with every charm illumes,*
> *At his command a new creation blooms,*
> *Born to grace nature and her works complete*
> *With all that's beautiful, sublime and great!*

ANON. (SEVENTEENTH CENTURY)

TOP LEFT: *A child's sandpit has been designed ingeniously to become a decorative part of this romantically planted garden.* (DESIGNER Michael Balston)

TOP RIGHT: *Brick-arched alcoves have been added to the walls of this small courtyard, to give a touch of depth and mystery.* (DESIGNERS Mathew West, Nigel Manton and Elizabeth Chandler)

~ 4 ~

HOW ART OF MAN CAN
PURCHASE NATURE AT A PRICE

Planting

Planting is the indispensable quickening element in gardens. It is like charity, 'the very bond of peace and all virtues', without which our terraces and tinkling fountains are nothing. Besides a knowledge of plants and flowers, it needs a sense of scale, a mature understanding of colour, deep reserves of patience and a degree of idiosyncrasy, amounting sometimes to prejudice, ready to break rules on occasions when doing so does not lead to anarchy.

A.D.B.WOODS

OPPOSITE: *Expertly contrasted foliage, including acer, acanthus, hosta, tradescantia and lamium, framing a lion-mask wall-fountain.* (DESIGNER David Ffrench)

IF PLANNING AND DESIGN ARE ENGROSSING, and construction satisfying, planting is the icing on the cake. Few things are more pleasurable than preparing the ground, dropping in the chosen plants and settling them there with a firm hand or heel. If plants are brought on from seed or cuttings, the euphoria is almost unbearable. But sentimentality is forbidden in a small garden, which is in many ways like an outsize container; there is no room for a careless accumulation of whatever takes the fancy. *Laissez-faire* will not do, every plant must earn its place in one way or another.

Nor should the plants have things all their own way: the garden may *seem* ebullient, but one must tie and train, tweak, pinch and prune or cut back without mercy to keep everything within bounds. If plants fail to thrive, are past their best or overgrow their allotted space, out they must come, no matter how dear to us; a good plant in the wrong place must also go or be shunted elsewhere.

'Half of gardening is self-control,' wrote Marion Cran (a prolific writer not usually afraid of hyperbole, but here almost succinct). 'Few garden-lovers start with the instinct to paint bold flower-scapes. They almost invariably plant a little of everything, to find that they have nothing in the end. The courage to fill a large space with one flower is seldom native to the beginner; it is won by mistakes and discontent, by experiment and failure, by the long teaching of time which makes artists of us all at last, and the unfortunate reflection obtrudes itself that by the time we have learned what to discard in life it is nearly time to discard life itself.'

56

But it is best to begin with the soil: where every plant is on permanent show, good soil will enable each to give of its best. Many grow in almost anything fertile, but others, infinitely desirable, are more demanding. Given the right planting medium, these will thrive in containers and raised beds – for a while, at least – but the garden soil, in the main, determines the plants we grow.

Some problems are obvious: sand, sticky clay, limestone and chalk are not difficult to spot, while acid soil is betrayed by the local presence of plants that thrive in it – camellias, rhododendrons, heathers and the rest. Garden centres sell inexpensive soil-testing kits that will remove any lingering doubts: these show the pH values of the soil, the degrees of alkalinity and acidity. A neutral soil gives a reading of pH 7; readings above this show an increasing degree of alkalinity, and those below, of acidity. A reading of somewhere between 6 and 7 pH denotes soil that will do for most purposes. In a large garden, you should take tests in several areas; in most small gardens the soil is likely to be of one type.

Then there is the soil structure: good soil is usually dark and crumbly with a clean, fresh smell to it. Not all gardens are so blessed, but it is possible to improve both the cold, claggy clays and the fast-draining, hungry sands, as well as the thin layers of topsoil often found over rock, chalk and limestone. All benefit from the same treatment – as much bulky, organic material as we can get: peat (or whenever possible, peat substitutes, bark, coir, etc.), well-rotted manures, leafmould, spent hops, seaweed, mushroom compost (not for acid-lovers), garden compost, etc. Clay takes all these plus masses of gravel and coarse grit. 'Grit, grit, lots of grit, the sharper the better. I now believe it to be one of the secrets of good gardening ... I got an Easter present (from myself to myself) of 5 cubic yards of this deliciously crumbly stuff...' wrote Vita Sackville-West, writer, gardener extraordinary and creator of the great garden at Sissinghurst in Kent.

Because of their cost, I give the sinister-sounding organic fertilizers (bonemeal, hoof and horn, dried blood, and blood, fish and bone) in small doses, and only to the most deserving plants, whereas my father kept vast stocks of them in the potting shed. Because it was off-limits, I still feel a touch of guilt when using them, as if caught tinkering with the communion wine: such is the abiding fascination of forbidden fruit.

No-dig gardening is appealing, especially for anyone with back trouble. Organic composts and fertilizers are applied to the surface and drawn down into the soil by the action of worms; thick mulches should then keep it moist, warm and relatively weed-free. Unfortunately birds, blackbirds especially in my garden, toss the mulch about, leaving bare patches in which weeds flourish – but then, that is a small price to pay for blackbirds.

Nevertheless, if the soil is poor, neglected or compacted, there is no substitute for digging, by at least one spit (spade's depth). This improves the soil structure and, like a cold shower, makes one feel virtuous when it is over. For uncultivated ground or where the drainage is poor, double-digging may be necessary, that is, excavating the soil to two spits deep. Remove perennial weeds, even the smallest bits of root. Fork over the subsoil at the bottom of the trench but do not let it be brought up and mixed with the topsoil. If the going is tough, hire a small, hand-operated mechanical rotovator for a few hours to loosen the soil; a mattock does the same job very well in a small area. Organic

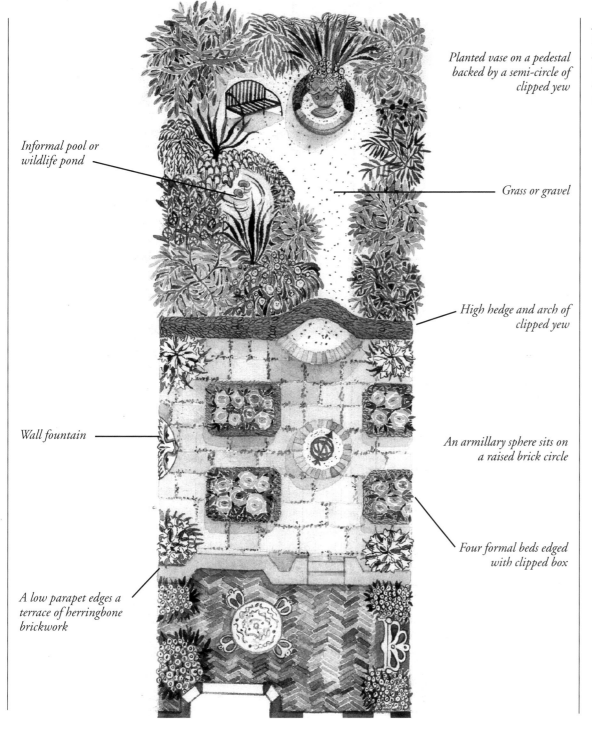

A formal design near the house leads, through an arch, to an informal area which could also be a child's playground or a vegetable plot.

Planted vase on a pedestal backed by a semi-circle of clipped yew

Informal pool or wildlife pond

Grass or gravel

High hedge and arch of clipped yew

Wall fountain

An armillary sphere sits on a raised brick circle

Four formal beds edged with clipped box

A low parapet edges a terrace of herringbone brickwork

matter (skimmed-off turf, garden compost, annual weeds, etc.) is thrown into the bottom of each trench.

Ideally, when the climate allows, it is best to dig in the autumn, allowing any winter frosts to break down the clods into crumbly soil. Life being what it is, do it whenever you can, except in wet weather when more harm than good would be done (compacting it even further), or in icy weather which is cruel on the spade-wielder. Leave the ground to settle, allowing the removal of any perennial weeds that reappear. Dig out perennial weeds and hoe off the annuals, or treat both with a contact weed-killer. All this work is repaid by healthy plants; in the restricted and somewhat artificial conditions available, they will appreciate all possible help.

In small gardens, particularly neglected town gardens (often little more than sour, impoverished cat-trays), it may be necessary to spend a fair amount of time and money on getting the ground in good heart. When short of money (and who is not when doing up a garden?) it pays to make trips to the country for such things as manure and leafmould, often free or relatively cheap there. Ask visiting friends to bring such things, infinitely more desirable than chocolates or wine.

Save all garden leaves in plastic sacks and stack to rot down out of sight, behind or under a bush. Homemade compost is excellent; there is room for a heap in all but the tiniest garden. All soft vegetable matter goes in, as long as it is not diseased, plus shredded paper, unravelled wool, sweepings, hair-trimmings, etc.; but fat and anything else of animal origin is absolutely out, except manure and urine, both of which can be added in small quantities, as accelerators. Place twiggy prunings and large tough leaves in a plastic bucket and chop with shears before adding to the heap. One is supposed to turn this over from time to time, but I forget and still get good results. A cubic yard or metre is a good size for a heap, but I have had perfectly satisfactory ones that were smaller. Bins are available from garden centres or by mail-order but one can make something passable from odd bits of wood.

Roses seem to like bananas and tea bags, whizzed in the blender: after a few doses, a Banksian rose of mine, barren for years, flowered its yellow head off. Seaweed is also free; when living in a small cottage by the coast we used to gather and spread barrow-loads of it over the clay subsoil at the bottom of each double-dug trench, and had the most magnificent sweet peas. Old mattresses were also popular in the area: first charred on a bonfire, then chopped up and dug into the soil, springs and all; the results seemed excellent.

Once the soil is ready, planting can begin. The framework of the garden is established before embarking on the detailed infilling. In *The Education of a Gardener*, Russell Page, the distinguished garden designer, describes a garden he would make for himself: 'But the garden's most usual livery is, after all, green, and I shall make it my main task to handle my plants and arrange them in their own terms of green. If I can succeed with groupings good in their forms, textures and differing tonalities, I shall be sure of harmony throughout the yearly rhythm of the garden. Then only I will consider flower colour as an added study and delight.' He follows this up withs a stern warning against the anaemic approach of some modern purists who, he reminds us, 'have pushed the theory of understatement in planting to ridiculous lengths.'

TREE AND TREE-LIKE SHRUBS FOR SMALL GARDENS

CONIFERS
(some will eventually grow too large, but are slow-growing and will do well for years)

Calocedrus decurrens Z7
Chamaecyparis lawsonia cvs.inc. 'Alumii', 'Columnaris', Kilmacurragh', 'Lane' 'Pembury Blue', 'Stewartii' and 'Wisellii' Z6
C. nootkatensis 'Pendula' Z5
C. obtusa 'Crippsii' Z6
Cupressus arizonica cvs. Z7
Juniperus communis 'Hibernica' Z7
J. scopulorum 'Skyrocket' Z3
Taxus baccata 'Fastigiata' Z6
T.b. 'Fastigiata Aurea' Z6

EVERGREENS
Acacia dealbata (mimosa) Z8
Arbutus unedo (strawberry tree) Z7
Camellia japonica cvs. Z7
C. x williamsii cvs. Z8
Ceanothus arboreus 'Trewithen Blue' Z9
Cordyline australis Z9
C. frigidus Z7
C. salicifolia 'Pendulus' Z6
C. simonsii Z5
Cytisus battandieri (Moroccan broom) Z7
Elaeagnus, to Z6
Embothrium coccineum Z7
Eucalyptus gunnii Z8
Eucryphia 'Nymansay' Z7
Euonymus, several, to Z7
Genista aetnensis (Mount Etna broom) Z7

Ilex aquifolium (English holly) cvs. inc 'Argentea Marginata' 'Argentea Marginata Pendula', 'Ferox Argentea', 'J.C. van Tol', 'Golden King', 'Golden Milkboy' and 'Silver Queen' Z7
I. opaca cvs. (American holly) Z5
I. x meservae, many cvs. (blue holly) Z6
Laurus nobilis, (bay tree) Z8
Ligustrum lucidum (privet) cvs. inc.L. 'Aureovariegatum', 'Excelsum Superbum' and 'Tricolor' Z7
L. sinense 'Variegatum' Z7
L. tschonoskii 'Vicaryi' Z6
Magnolia grandiflora, small cvs. Z7
Photinia davidiana (stranvaesia) Z7
Trachycarpus fortunei (Chusan palm, windmill palm) Z9

DECIDUOUS
Acer griseum (paper bark maple) Z5
A. negundo 'Variegatum' and A.n. 'Flamingo' Z7
A. palmatum Z5 many cvs. inc A. 'Atropurpureum', *Acer palmatum* 'Bloodgood', 'Butterfly', dissectum, 'Osakazuki'and 'Sango-kaku' (coral bark maple) Z5
A. pseudoplatanus 'Brilliantissimum' Z5
A. shirasawanum aureum Z6
Aralia elata (Japanese angelica tree) and A.e.'Variegata' Z4
Betula pendula 'Youngii' (weeping birch) Z1
Caragana arborescens 'Lobergii' (Siberian pea) Z2

C.a. 'Walker' Z2
Catalpa bignonioides (Indian bean tree) Z5
C.b. 'Aurea' Z5
Cercidiphyllum japonicum Z5
Cercis siliquastrum (Judas tree) Z6
C. canadensis 'Forest Pansy' Z4
Cornus alternifolia 'Argentea ' Z3
C. kousa Z5
Cotinus coggygria cvs. inc 'Flame' C.g. 'Notcutt's Variety and 'Royal Purple'
Cotinus obovatus Z5
Crataegus (hawthorn) most, to Z5
Elaeagnus angustifolia (Russian olive) Z2
Gleditsia triacanthos 'Sunburst' and G.t. 'Rubylace' Z3
Hydrangea paniculata 'Grandi flora' Z3
Magnolia, many, inc:
M. cylindrica Z6
M. x loebneri 'Leonard Messel' and 'Merrill' Z5
M. salicifolia 'Wada's Memory' Z6
M. soulangeana cvs. Z5
M. stellata Z5
Mahonia, most, inc:
M. lomarifolia Z7
M. x media 'Buckland' Z7
M. 'Charity' Z7
Malus (crab-apple), most, inc:
M. coronaria 'Charlottae 'Z4
M. 'Eleyi' Z4
M. floribunda, Z4
M. 'John Downie'
M. 'Profusion'
M. pumila 'Dartmouth' Z3
M. 'Red Jade' (weeping)

M. robusta 'Red Sentinel' Z3
M. 'Royalty'
M. sargentii Z4
M. sieboldii Z5
M. tschonoskii Z4
M. 'Van Esseltine' Z6
M. x zumi 'Golden Hornet' Z5
Prunus 'Amanogawa'
P. 'Spire' Z6
P. incisa, cvs. Z6
P. mume 'Beni-chidori' Z6
P. 'Okumiyako'
P. 'Pendula Rubra'
P. pendula 'Pendula Rosea'
P. 'Taihaku'
P. x subhirtella 'Autumnalis' Z5
P. x s 'Autumnalis Rosea' Z5
P. triloba Z5
Pyrus salicifolia 'Pendula' (weeping silver pear) Z4
Rhus typhina (stag's-horn sumach) and R.t. 'Dissecta' Z3
Salix caprea 'Kilmarnock' Z5
S. exigua Z2
S. purpurea 'Pendula' Z5
Sophora japonica 'Pendula 'Z5
Sorbus aria 'Lutescens' Z5
S. hupehensis Z6
S. 'Joseph's Rock Z6
S. vilmorinii Z6
Tamarix ramosissima (tamarisk) Z2
T. tetrandra Z6

BULBS AND CORMS

Allium (ornamental garlic)
Anemone
Arum italicum
Chionodoxa
Convallaria (lily of the valley)
Crinum
Crocus
Cyclamen coum
C. hederifolium
Eranthis hyemalis (winter aconite)

Erythronium dens-canis (dog's tooth violet)
Eucomis
Fritillaria pyrenaica (fritillary)
Galanthus (snowdrop)
Hyacinthoides hispanica (Spanish bluebell)
H. non-scripta (bluebell)
Hyacinthus (hyacinth)
Iris

Leucojum (snowflake)
Lilium (lily)
Muscari (grape hyacinth)
Narcissus (daffodil)
N. bulbocodium and cvs.
N. cyclamineus and cvs.
N. triandrus triandrus (angel's tears) and cvs. inc 'April Tears', 'February Gold', 'February Silver', 'Hawera', 'Jack

Snipe', 'Jenny', 'Liberty Bells', 'Peeping Tom' and 'Tête-à-Tête', *N.* 'Thalia'
Polygonatum (Solomon's seal)
Puschkiniana scilloides
Scilla sibirica
Tulipa

Although a wide range of plant material is obtainable these days, such are the enormous differences in climate and conditions in even quite a small area that it is wise find out the hardiness and requirements of any plant with which we have fallen in love. A good, up-to-date plant encyclopaedia which gives the climate zones or degrees of frost-hardiness for each plant is worth having or borrowing. Most of the better plant catalogues and gardening magazines now give reasonably detailed information about the likes and dislikes of the plants described.

Plants that are an integral part of the basic design form the bones or skeleton of the garden. Some, frequently evergreen, with strong form and striking foliage, we call architectural, and these add drama: *Rhus typhina, Fatsia, Magnolia, Acanthus* and *Yucca* are good examples of architectural plants. Evergreens and plants with a sculptural shape are especially important in winter, standing out when others are bare or unremarkable. Well-grouped plants have a similar effect; by positioning an upright tree alongside a spreading, horizontal shrub, or a rounded bush with something spiked, satisfying contrasts and balances are made.

Other, less individually imposing plants, when *en masse*, can play an equally decisive part, as visual 'stops', buttresses, windbreaks, ground cover, hedges and so on. Hedges enclose a garden in a definitive green frame which stamps its authority on the design; internal hedges used for screens and partitions also have an important influence. Before deciding on clipped hedges, ask who will have enough time or patience to trim them regularly. Garden centres and many small outfits offer maintenance at a price: if they know what they are doing, the price is probably worth paying, but if the lawn is mown and edged, and weeding done too, costs mount up.

A well-grown hedge is a handsome thing and an effective wind-filter. It blots out some of the surrounding cacophony, but takes up a fair amount of space even when clipped severely. Too tall a hedge towers over us, so the height must be in proportion to the whole. Hedges are excellent disguises for ugly fences; ivy does the same job in much less space if controlled from the start. A cheap wire fence covered in ivy or something similar soon makes a neat boundary if the plants are fed, watered and trimmed regularly.

Look around and see which plants make satisfactory hedges in near-by gardens. In many areas, yew is the best of hedges; indifferent to soil, noble all year long, and a good backdrop. Grown well, it reaches a reasonable size in seven to ten years. Beech makes a neat hedge; the young leaves are delicious and age with dignity as they turn to russet, in which state they cling on till spring; some dislike this – a matter of taste, or of past associations, no doubt. Hornbeam is not dissimilar; its branches may be trained and clipped along or over a frame until they are entwined and strong enough to form living rails or tunnels. Both beech and hornbeam grow, if not quite at a lick, at least at a reasonable pace if you treat them well, and succeed virtually anywhere in a temperate climate.

Holly is excellent. Close to the house, plant smooth-leaved varieties; their foliage is neatly lustrous and not unpleasant to handle when pruning or tidying. Most are very hardy: English holly (*Ilex aquifolium*), American holly (*I. opaca*), and Japanese holly (*I. crenata*) all do well in towns and cities. Hawthorn is charming: even when hard-clipped it has an informal feel to it, but is as tough as can be; although the leaves fall eventually, it will still be dense and impenetrable. Yellow privet,

OPPOSITE TOP: *The variegated form of* Fatsia japonica. *The shiny, deeply-cut leaves of this handsome, shade-tolerant evergreen shrub make it invaluable in many situations.* (DESIGNER Angela Kirby)

OPPOSITE BOTTOM: *A magnificent specimen of* Acer rubrum *'October Glory', showing the glowing colour and finely dissected foliage.*

although unfashionable, is jolly and puts up with neglect, poor soil and pollution; I like it enormously, but it is a greedy feeder and needs two or three clips a year. For the small front gardens of cottages, a castellated hedge of privet or hawthorn, or one that has birds, teapots and other fancies bursting out at the top, is fun; it is possible to become bored with too much good taste, to long for something altogether more rumbustious.

In the milder parts of temperate regions, especially near the sea, escallonias make attractive evergreen hedges and excellent windbreaks, as they will survive salt-laden gales. *Escallonia rubra* 'Crimson Spire' is a good one, but there are many others. Inland, I have found them to be pretty tough; we had some ancient ones in a garden which was about 800 feet (250m) above sea level and subject to frequent severe winters (for England), so one could hardly call it sheltered. Less hardy, *Escallonia* 'Iveyi' is a charmer: an upright grower, with oval, glossy leaves of dark green setting off the small, fragrant white flowers. Escallonias prefer sun, but 'Iveyi' grows well enough on a shaded wall in my present garden.

These same plants are used to divide up a longer garden into smaller units, but if something lower, yet still formal, is required, box (boxwood) is excellent. *Buxus sempervirens* reaches ten feet (3m) or more eventually, if allowed to do so, and is sometimes seen as a great, billowing tunnel in old gardens. *B.s.* 'Handsworthiensis' is another tall grower, while *B.s.* 'Suffruticosa' is perfect for a low edging; there are many others. Intricate patterns and 'knots' are made by using plain green box in conjunction with another that has variegated or different-toned leaves.

Small, formal beds edged by low hedges are delightful for roses, herbs and seasonal bedding; clipped box, lavender, silvery *Santolina chamaecyparissus*, *Berberis buxifolia* 'Nana', and the purple-leaved *Berberis thunbergii* 'Atropurpurea Nana' are good, and I imagine the small yellow holly with tiny leaves, *Ilex crenata* 'Golden Gem', might do very well. These little hedges make good frames round pots, pools, statues and small standard trees, and such combinations are excellent for neat, low-maintenance front gardens.

Low 'step-over' edgings of espalier-trained fruit trees are only one branch high, and look demure beside a narrow path or around a bed where herbs, vegetables, saladings and standard fruit bushes grow; with spring blossom, summer leaves, fruit in autumn and gnarled winter branches, they earn their keep. Taller espaliers and fans three or four branches high make good garden dividers and are decorative on walls.

Whatever the hedging plants, the preparation of the ground will be much the same as for other trees and shrubs, but is more easily done if a well-dug trench is prepared, with plenty of organic matter. Give container-grown plants a trench about twice as wide as their container, and bare-rooted plants one wide enough to allow their roots to be well spread. Make the trenches deep enough to ensure that when the plants are firmed in, the replaced earth finishes at the same level as the original soil-line on the plants. After this, a good soaking followed by a two-inch (5cm) mulch of some kind should get the young plants growing strongly. An annual feed and one or two trimmings each year ensure that the hedge is healthy, shapely and well covered by leaves from the base upwards.

After the hedges come the specimen plants and other important plant groupings. Plant those chosen for shelter, privacy and screening first. Whether they are evergreen, deciduous, or a mixture of both, will depend to some extent on the problem. When some unsightly thing is clearly visible from the house after the leaves fall, it is best to choose an evergreen. If, on the other hand, it can be seen only from the garden or if the main need for privacy comes mainly when dining or sunbathing, a deciduous tree or shrub will protect us during those months when we are likely to be out there long enough to care about it very much, yet allow light into the garden during the winter months.

I planted a fast-growing yellow robinia, *Robinia pseudoacacia* 'Frisia', to screen a horribly mutilated apple tree in the garden of the house opposite and a monstrous water-tank on its roof. Beneath it I added two *Elaeagnus pungens* 'Maculata'. Soon 'Rambling Rector' (a neighbour's nomadic white rose) and my own blue clematis 'Mrs Cholmondeley' threaded their way between. In less than three years this group blotted out both offenders, while as a bonus, the lawn was thick with robinia seedlings, bright and perky as a flock of tiny yellow parrots. This tree has brittle branches, so it is fine for a screen but not for a windbreak.

The winter-flowering cherry *Prunus* x *subhirtella* 'Autumnalis' does the same job rather more delicately: what it lacks in summer *brio*, it makes up for with its fragile-looking blossom during the bleaker months. Whether for use, or merely for decoration, when room can be found for only one tree, this treasure is difficult to resist. It is hard to make a final choice, for the minute the virtues of one are decided upon, the merits of another will not be denied.

I would be sad not to have at least one of the small crab-apples, and at a pinch, would settle on *Malus floribunda,* so smothered in spring with carmine buds opening to blush-white blossom, that an angelic cloud appears to hover over the garden. Or there is *Malus coronaria* 'Charlottae', whose pink double flowers smell deliciously of violets. But for jelly, I find the best are 'John Downie', 'Golden Hornet' or little 'Red Glow', with pink flowers and striking red fruit.

Flowering cherries also are nearly irresistible. *Prunus* 'Taihaku' has the largest white flowers and is a wonderful sight in spring, but can grow to twenty feet or more high and wide (6 x 6m), so is really best for the larger end of the small-garden range. Rather smaller and perhaps even lovelier is *Prunus* 'Okumiyako' (*P. serrulata* 'Longipes'), rightly described by Brigadier Lucas Phillips in *The Small Garden* as 'tenderly beautiful'; from its spreading branches dangle large, double, white flowers. *Prunus* 'Amanogawa', on the other hand, is sometime sneered at for the coarseness of its leaves after the flowers have fallen, but when in spring the columnar branches are wreathed (admittedly for a short time) in scented, pale pink blossom I can forgive it practically anything. It takes up very little room and I rather like the fallen petals that swirl and drift about the garden, just as briefly beautiful on the ground as when blushing delicately on the branches. Where wind is a problem, the silver sea buckthorn (*Hippophae rhamnoides*) is an excellent plant and a useful screen; the orange-red berries are jolly, but you need male and female plants.

The evergreen *Rhamnus alaternus* 'Argenteovariegata' is a useful, fast-growing shrub, excellent in temperate regions, both by the sea and in cities; its grey-green leaves, edged with white, give it a soft, silvery appearance. Billowing up to about ten feet (3m) high and rather less wide, it makes a rapid, decorous screen, either on its own or at the back of a border, with a rose like 'Cornelia' clambering through its branches. It is also good for quick topiary work, as recommended by London and Wise in *The Retired Gardener'* (1706): '... give it what shape you think fit, by the help of your shears, which being well-guided, will make of this shrub a very agreeable figure'.

It is tempting to plant *Eucalyptus gunnii* as a quick 'everblue' screen; it grows so speedily, even from quite a small specimen, that in three or four years it is a charming little tree. Alas, it does not know when to stop, for it then rushes on at an alarming rate and soon outgrows a small garden. If you should have room, it will certainly screen out most things, all year long, in a remarkably efficient way, but I prefer to use it ornamentally by cutting it down regularly nearly to ground level in late spring or early summer, which keeps it within bounds and ensures that the leaves remain in their pretty, juvenile form. A hard frost may cut these plants down, but they often sprout again.

The privets are more biddable, and soon reach a useful height. They are so accommodating; mostly evergreen (or semi-evergreen in harsh conditions), and being wind-, shade- and pollution-tolerant, and grow almost anywhere (although those with yellow leaves lose some their brightness in shade). I love the smell of privet, too; it is as redolent of summer, in its sweetish, foxy way, as any rose, but some people detest the smell, so sniff before buying. Of those I have grown, *Ligustrum lucidum* is superb, with camellia-like leaves and panicles of white flowers in autumn. *Ligustrum lucidum* 'Excelsum Superbum' is a lovely thing, too: its leaves are splashed softly with yellow and cream, giving a very subtle effect. Although privets are notoriously rapacious, I have never had any trouble with this one, or with the rather similar 'Tricolor', whose narrower leaves have a white margin and are tipped with pink when young. As for the yellow privets, so often straitjacketed by strict pruning, they take on a quite a new character when allowed to grow unclipped, becoming bright and pleasantly blowzy little trees in time, often developing interesting trunks and branches as they age. There is the familiar golden privet, *Ligustrum ovalifolium* 'Aureum', and also *L.* 'Vicaryi', which is the best, I think.

Before deciding on the final positioning of whatever trees have been chosen, remember the neighbours whose gardens border ours: we may be entitled to plant where we choose, but it is not kind to deprive them of light or ruin their views.

Once the necessary shelter and privacy are achieved, it is the turn of the other plants that will figure prominently in the garden. In a very small garden, there may be room for only one, so it should be a stunner. It would be perfectly sensible to spend a fair sum on an outstanding plant or piece of topiary: an aralia, Japanese maple, camellia, box (boxwood) cones and spirals, a pair of mop-headed *Elaeagnus pungens* 'Maculata' or blue *Cupressus arizonica glabra*. Any of these, initially expensive, might prove a positive economy, having such an impact that very little else would be needed.

Standard roses are charming in a small garden: some, like 'Canary Bird', flower in just one spectacular flush (but have attractive, fern-like foliage for the rest of the season); others, like 'The Fairy', repeat generously till Christmas. Standard hybrid teas are, I think, a little too top-heavy to be attractive here, but some of the more delicate shrub and cluster-flowered roses make perfect centre-pieces for formal beds or will line up beside a path. Both 'Ballerina' and 'Yesterday' have small flowers and will 'come again'. They, or one or two quarter-standards of the little pompon rose 'White

Pet', would be very fetching in even the tiniest front garden. In a larger plot, old-fashioned weeping standards such as 'Félicité Perpétue', 'Albéric Barbier' and 'François Juranville' swoon over their galvanized-metal frames with an almost indecent languor at midsummer. Roses and other prickly plants make good centrepieces for the front garden, less likely to be stolen than a handsome container or statue.

Standard wisterias are infinitely desirable. They need sun to flower really well, bearing long, scented racemes of white, mauve or purple flowers in summer; in winter their twisted branches have rugged charm. A pair of them on either side of a bench is a delicious extravagance; if you train them yourself, they will be little more expensive than anything else. Let a young stem twist round a stout stake, which is removed when the wisteria as grown strong enough to support itself; this makes an interesting-looking plant. For shade, grow honeysuckle and ivy in the same fashion, both charming in a modest way, and it does not take too long to grow fast-moving golden privet into a jolly standard.

Although most towns now have garden centres, the country usually produces cheaper plants and specialist nurseries for the more unusual things. Mail-order is necessary for most of us. Many

Clematis montana clambering over a garden trellis. It can also be grown over walls, railings and fences and allowed to tumble down slopes or to drape itself over any large shrub or tree to great effect. (1-8 Malvern Terrace, London)

firms are very reliable but with others (including, I fear, some famous names) it is a bit of a lottery, particularly with roses, when some wretched thing is high-handedly substituted, without apology, for the superior creature one has ordered.

Use a pair or several pairs of plants in many ways around the garden. At the corners of a terrace, for instance, to mark a flight of steps, by a front porch or an archway, at bends in a flower bed, or planted asymmetrically along the garden, thus drawing the eye to and round them into areas beyond.

The repeated use of plants in a garden has a unifying effect. Topiary cones and slender upright conifers are useful here, taking up little room but making neat exclamation marks among the lower, rounded plants. Placing a single architectural plant as the object of attention at the end of a path, or as a centrepoint in the garden (or part of one), helps to focus a design. A plant set at the side and some way down a small garden again pulls the eye along and round.

Roses, clematis and other climbers (vines), grown over arches, arbours, pergolas, tunnels and obelisks, make a strong contribution to a design, but such structures need careful placing and must seem logical: giving shelter, marking a change of level or establishing the transition from one part of the garden to another. In a narrow side garden (sideyard), a pergola or tunnel across it makes an attractive and sheltered seating area, screening out any unattractive buildings near by. A pair of tunnels or pergolas, placed over paths that run down each side of a wider garden, giving shade and shelter, also looks natural and necessary; place an urn, statue or a seat at the end of each, for the eye to rest on. Arches plumped down in an arbitrary fashion seems lonely and ridiculous, but when leading to an enclosed space or framing a view they are most effective.

Nothing could be more romantic than a bower draped with wisteria and roses. I saw a village garden where a circular arbour of stout posts was set round an old well-head. It supported two free-flowering wisterias which had formed twisted columns and a latticed roof. The yellow-splashed ivy 'Goldheart' (syn. *Hedera* 'Oro di Bogliasco') grew up each post, so that even in winter it was a striking sight. In summer it became a green tent studded with purple scented flowers, charming to sit in, the well's broad rim making a cool seat.

When planting along a wall, consider its aspect, materials and colour. Designing a garden for a house in the north of England which she had not seen, Jekyll wrote to the builders on site to ask what material was being used for the construction, and the exact tone, 'whether it is a cool grey, like Portland stone after weathering, or a warmer colour?' and was sent a sample of stone in reply (and samples of the soil and subsoil too); such attention to detail is admirable. While a white or pastel-washed wall will accept plants of virtually any colour, new, harsh brickwork has to be treated carefully, for the more staring the bricks, the more they must be softened by plants of a sympathetic colour. Ivy does a splendid job on most walls, while yellow walls are helped by blues, purples, other yellows, white and dark green. I have seen the near-evergreen rose 'Mermaid' doing a marvellous job on such a wall, sprawling across it with the coppery tints of the young shoots, the dark green of the mature leaves and the large single yellow flowers with their amber centres all flattering the brickwork wonderfully.

Graham Stuart Thomas, in *The Art of Planting*, suggests white, yellow, blue and purple flowers with red brick, but there are no absolute rules: with so many shades of red and yellow, so many mottled bricks, and so many degrees of weathering, experiments must be made.

Mellowed stone and weathered bricks are much easier to deal with, but even these look better if plants are chosen to enhance them. Using watercolours, it is easy enough to paint some paper with a wash that matches the colour of the house walls and then try scraps of various colours against it, to find the right partners; the colours of leaves, flowers and fruit are all taken into account.

Wooden houses are best kept free of climbers (vines) to allow for repainting, but if such plants are used, they may be tied to special nails or kept in place by the new adhesive-backed plastic ties, so that they can be pulled away carefully when necessary. If trellis panels are fitted, it is best to fit hinges along the bottom edges and a latch at the top, so allowing the panels and the attached plants to be pulled gently away from the wall during repainting. Alternatively, grow free-standing shrubs in nearby beds or in containers at the foot of the walls. Allow a few climbing plants (vines) on the pillars of any porches, verandahs and balconies there may be or grow them near by on arches, hoops, obelisks and trellis screens.

For the rest of the garden, plants grouped in containers, beds and borders will put flesh on the bones. Here the blending or contrasting of shades, shapes and textures is important. It is difficult to get everything right at first, even if the theory is impeccable, for nature and chance will take a hand; frosts come too late or too early, nurseries supply mislabelled specimens, one plant mysteriously fails while another recklessly self-seeds, industrious dogs dig up a prized specimen and the birds ravish something we value especially. Sometimes the theory *is* at fault: what looked so right on paper turns out to be boring, clichéd or just plain horrid in practice, but one tries again, until it all comes right.

Slight changes and repositioning will often do the trick. It is easy to fall into the trap of doing what seems obviously sensible, putting the tallest plants at the back, the medium-sized ones in the middle, and the smallest in front, but then the plants look like boot-faced boys in a school photograph. We must pull Brown major out and forward, or even to the front, at the same time pushing Smith mimimus and some of his friends back into the middle row, among Robinson minor's gang, several of whom then surge forward to fill the resulting gaps.

It is a mistake to think that a small garden should have only the smallest plants: one or two large specimens with outsize leaves are more dramatic than a whole collection of dinky little things. There is a town house near me which has a narrow, gravelled courtyard and just one plant, the Japanese angelica tree (*Aralia elata*), its huge, pinnate leaves throwing great shadows on the white walls and gravelled floor. The owner rightly refrains from adding anything more.

Another house, in a quiet corner of a large city, has a cobbled front garden with the Indian bean tree (*Catalpa bignonioides*) at its centre, rather large for such a small area, but very striking there, and that too is all, except for a pair of antique vases of white petunias at each side of the porch. Both the aralia and the catalpa lose their foliage in autumn, but the exotic loquat, *Eriobotrya japonica*, keeps its corrugated leaves throughout the year, and in a hot summer has clusters of fragrant flowers followed by edible fruit. It is frost-hardy in the mild, sheltered areas of temperate zones

The exotic-looking foliage of Canna *'King Humbert'*, Canna *'Wyoming'* and ligularia *in designer Myles Challis's London garden.*

and there is a magnificent specimen in my daughter's small garden in London.

The designer and plantsman Myles Challis has shown how just how effective giant, exotic-looking plants like rheums and gunneras can be in a limited space; despite the climate, his narrow London garden is planted with a tropical generosity. Something similar could be tried more often. In a tiny garden, a clump of the spiky New Zealand flax, *Phormium tenax*, rising from a pool of round-leaved bergenias would be a good combination of contrasting shapes.

The use of colour is possibly the most difficult of garden arts. Sylvia Crowe advised approaching it in one of three ways: in the first, a garden is designed in monotone, with a few high-notes of colour; the second follows the laws and patterns of nature; while the third, most difficult way is to treat the plants as colours on a palette with which to 'paint' the garden. In the first case, there might be a skeleton of clipped evergreens, with the addition of a few colourful plants in pots. In the second, blends that occur in nature are chosen: the yellows, whites, blues and fresh greens of spring, followed by summer shades of mauve, pinks and deeper blues, with occasional hot spots of red and purple, softened by silver, among the dark green foliage. Last would come the bronze, orange, yellow and scarlet of autumn. For the third and hardest way, the eye of an artist must combine with the skill and knowledge of a plant expert.

Sunlight drains colour, with the result that the pure, strong colours that look right under a fierce sun often seem harsh in more temperate areas, but that does not mean that only soft, muted colours and pastel shades can be used there; it could be argued that those who live in a cooler climate need warmth and brightness all the more. Hot reds, yellows and orange; reddish-purple and deep pinks; rich russet and polished bronze, these colours will bring a glow to the garden, while blues, greens, mauves, greys and silvers will cool it. White flowers sparkle and at dusk seem luminous. In daylight, however, too much white looks stark and unsettling, but drifts of cream and ivory, together with the 'blush' tones and the soft, greenish or silvery near-whites found in such plants as crambe, astrantia and gypsophila, are altogether easier on the eye, and together with green and silver foliage,

BOTTOM LEFT: *The winter aconite,* Eranthis hyemalis *'Guinea Gold', lights up many a gloomy corner in the early months.*

BOTTOM RIGHT: *Lily, nicotiana, helichrysum and oxalis in their summer splendour.*

make good buffer-zones between colourful groups that might otherwise quarrel.

Much can be learnt by playing with a colour-wheel and with paint sample-cards. By grouping the cards in various ways, and against backgrounds of different greens (or the colours of the garden furniture and the house walls), it becomes clear how one colour or group of colours enhances or detracts from another. Fashion in colour comes and goes as in all else, but one should be leery of it in the garden, for it can have a deadening hand. There are really no bad or good colours, bad or good plants, just a trite or unskilful use of them; one day I shall do something very subtle with red salvias.

Few small gardens have the length and breadth needed for the herbaceous borders of old, and few of us would want either the work they involved or the stretches of almost bare earth from late

A wonderful spring tapestry of tulips, hyacinths, grape-hyacinths, pansies and aubrieta on an Oxfordshire rockery. (Mrs Frank's garden, Steeple Aston, Oxfordshire)

autumn to spring. A mixed border is more like it, with deciduous and evergreen (or silver, or gold) plants blended with roses, perennials, annuals and bulbs, a good proportion of them scented; without scent a garden is a poor thing.

Bright, stimulating colours are better kept near to the house, with the softer shades melting away towards the boundaries. There is also the shape and texture of foliage to consider: setting the round leaf against the sword, the glossy against the matt, the smooth against the corrugated, and so on, for all add to the garden tapestry.

' ... The thing that matters is that, in its season, the border should be kept full and beautiful, by what means does not matter in the least,' (Jekyll again) and this advice may be followed in the rest of the garden as well. A quiet corner, perhaps in a not too-shaded side passage, will house a succession of bulbs, perennials and annuals in pots, grown on to fill any gaps. In this way, one can keep the garden at near-perfection throughout the year. Bought-in plants do the same job, although this is expensive and cheating. But then, cheating is often necessary in a small garden.

> *The world's a garden, pleasures are the flowers,*
> *Of fairest hues, in form and member many,*
> *The lily, first, pure-whitest flower of any,*
> *Rose sweetest fair, with pinkèd gilliflowers*
> *The violet, and the double marigold,*
> *And pansy too, but after all mischances,*
> *Death's winter comes and kills with sudden cold,*
> *Rose, lily, violet, marigold, pink, pansies.*

JOSUAH SYLVESTER (1563–1618)

~ 5 ~

TO THE GARDEN GLORIOUS

The Sunny Garden

Who that has reason and his smell
Would not amongst rose and jasmine dwell,
Rather than all his spirits choke
With exhalations of dirt and smoke.

ABRAHAM COWLEY (1618–67)

OPPOSITE: *A beautifully confident handling of colour in the planting of this sun-filled garden, seen here in full fig during the summer months.* (DESIGNER Sue Berger)

IT HAS AN UP-TO-DATE RING; was there really such pollution in the 1600s? Little changes: we still need to retreat from the unfriendly streets and where better than into a secret, sunny garden? In cold climates, many of us only survive winter by dreaming of the glories of summer to come; if the dreams fail to materialize, we fall into a depression.

In temperate climates, those of us whose gardens face the sun have the best of things: a warm terrace just outside the door, walls where the tenderest plants may grow, and the perfect conditions for a pool full of waterlilies and goldfish, or one fed by a gleaming fall of water.

It may seem tempting to place a conservatory here between house and terrace, but, even in cooler regions, a sunny conservatory at midday in summer can be unbearably hot: plants and humans will shrivel unless there are efficient shades. On the other hand, a conservatory which catches the morning or evening sun is pleasant for those out at work all day.

A sunny terrace gets a lot of use so should be as large as possible. Any form of paving or ground surfacing will do here, for moss and algae are unlikely to be a problem. Marble looks chilly in cool climates but seems entirely at home in hotter regions. Brick, slate or stone is ideal for many houses, soaking up the daytime warmth until the terrace becomes a giant storage-heater, a delicious place to walk on at night, barefoot. These all allow small plants to grow in gaps between them, but do not overdo it; the serenity of the terrace is lost if it is covered by a rash of plants and there is the danger of tripping over the clumps in an unguarded moment.

When marble, stone and even brick are too expensive, gravel does very well, for its neutral tones reflect little of the sun's glare (white gravel should be avoided here for that reason). In less formal gardens, plants grow and seed themselves about in gravel, yet weeds are easily pulled up or kept at bay by a couple of applications of weedkiller during the growing season.

Wooden surfaces are unlikely to become slippery in the sun. Old boards look rugged with both contemporary architecture and the informal ambience of seaside or cottage gardens: it is always pleasant to do a little recycling. Decking and railway sleepers (cross-ties) are also agreeable. All of these go well with cobblestones, pebbles, shingle and gravel.

In a seaside town I visited recently there was an unusual, sunny small garden that was remarkably attractive and labour-saving. Climbers (vines) sprawled on the walls; at their feet was a wide stone terrace with battered cane furniture set among pots of white geraniums and grey leaves. Beyond lay undulating drifts of cobblestones which sprouted silver clumps of sea buckthorn, pink wisps of tamarisk, more silver-grey plants and a few tussocks of thrift. In one corner, an old boat sank gently through the stones beside a black anchor; beyond the end wall lay the pebbled beach and the sea. Not a difficult garden to copy and perfect for those with little spare time. Something similar could be done in an inland garden with sculpture or some rural artefact replacing the boat and anchor.

I once made a garden on the sunny side of a small cottage, designed for weekenders with limited time and money. The borders were edged by old stones from a demolished privy, gravel covered the remaining ground and an ancient roller was both useful and ornamental. Shrubs hid the inexpensive wooden fencing panels and a few small trees gave a little shade to the garden without taking too much sun from the neighbours. Quick-growing plants filled the borders, so weeding was unnecessary and they had been chosen to look after themselves, with no staking and very little pruning. As the water-table was high, watering was not much of a problem. The gravel was raked occasionally and given the odd dose of weed-killer. With remarkably little effort the garden remained pretty throughout the year in a simple, unsophisticated way that suited the cottage.

Even in the sun, wind can be troublesome, whistling through side passages or gusting with cold devastation through gaps in the surrounding buildings; then we must protect the garden – or at least the most vital parts of it – but without shutting out the sun. Short wing-walls, jutting out just far enough to shield the terrace, are one answer: about eight feet (2.5m) high by the depth of the terrace, built to match the house walls. These also provide more space for climbers (vines) and tender plants. A run of extra-high trellis or palings alongside the terrace will do a similar job, rather more cheaply.

There are those who love the sun but can stand only just so much of it; for them, build a second paved area, if there is shade in one part of the garden, or some kind of shelter, preferably near to the house. In hot climates, a loggia, a wide, pillared porch, verandah or even a covered balcony would be handsome.

Something more temporary is often enough in a small garden. Sun-blinds are cheerful; they pull out to shade a bench or a small table and some chairs, yet the house is not deprived of light on duller days. In a front garden where alterations are prohibited, as well as in any of the smallest plots, a large parasol or sun-umbrella is ideal, moved around to shade chairs and tables. Their canvas should not do battle with the flowers: plain shades of off-white, cream or ecru are charming, with just a hint of colonial dash to them. These colours are also good for any washable cushions and chair-covers in the garden, though for sheer practicality, especially if small children are about, dark colours, plain or chequered, would probably be better.

One might plant a tree or large shrub on or just beside the terrace to throw a little shade when it is most needed. Most medium-sized specimens will do. Those that give a broken or lightly dappled shade are particularly welcome, but their eventual size must also be kept in mind lest the whole area becomes deprived of sun. Many of the small to medium-sized trees mentioned earlier are ideal here, but there are plenty of others; if they should be scented, so much the better.

I like the pineapple-scented Moroccan broom (*Cytisus battandieri*), which has silver-green leaves and lemon-yellow flowers in summer: it can be pinched and pruned to keep it within bounds.

The pineapple-scented Moroccan broom, Cytisus battandieri, *ceanothus and poppies growing against a sunny wall. (Greenhurst Garden, Sussex)*

That wonderful evergreen, *Ceanothus arboreus* 'Trewithen Blue', quickly grows large enough to stand in for a small tree; with glossy leaves and a smothering of blue flowers, it is a lovely thing.

Even quicker, the deciduous *Acer negundo* 'Flamingo' shoots up at amazing speed; its green leaves are softly variegated with white and pink, giving it a delicate appearance which is belied by its vigour, for in my last garden I had to cut it back quite ruthlessly each spring, a treatment it did not mind at all.

A seat beneath a tree is pleasant: it might be a canvas chair, a bench or one of those circular affairs fixed round the trunk. Ancient fruit trees are sometimes found in old gardens and even in new ones which are built on the sight of a previous orchard. These are perfect for a shady seat as long as there are not too many over-ripe fruit to fall on the unsuspecting head, but even a newly planted fruit tree will soon grow large enough to provide a little shelter; choose one grown on a dwarfing rootstock so that it does not get above itself.

The evergreen *Magnolia grandiflora* is a noble sight against a house: the creamy flowers are ravishing – great, heavily scented goblets. They do well on sunny walls in warm and sheltered areas and are perfectly happy in the city, while I have seen a grand old specimen growing on the side of a house by the coast, seemingly unmoved by the salt-laden winds it receives from time to time. The American-born garden designer Lanning Roper suggested that magnolias might survive in colder parts if grown on a chimney wall, and this could be worth trying, but now that most houses are centrally heated, all the house walls give out useful warmth in winter, so perhaps the chimney is unnecessary. The varieties 'Exmouth' and 'Goliath' flower at an early age, but all magnolias bestow an unrivalled *cachet* on the garden. In favoured zones they can be grown quite happily as free-standing specimens.

A fig tree would be a possibility: they grow to quite a size, but the leaves throw a beautifully patterned shade, and if the roots are kept confined, they fruit more freely (as a child, I was told they were planted in the belly of a dead pig). 'Brown Turkey' is still the one to try: in a very small garden, fan-train it against a wall.

The strawberry tree (*Arbutus unedo*) is a good evergreen for this situation; in temperate climates it is hardy by the sea and in sheltered areas inland; it grows to twenty feet (6m) in time, but takes many years to do so. If and when it outgrows its welcome, probably we shall be past caring. It is shrubby-looking to begin with, but can be pruned to give it a definite trunk. The small white flowers appear in autumn among the strawberry-like fruit (which are tasteless, but quite edible, so that there are no worries if the children eat them). I have grown a strawberry tree for many years in a large pot, taking it with me from garden to garden; it is still just possible to move it around as my schemes change, but perhaps it now deserves to be pensioned off and allowed to grow old gracefully in the open ground. Many plants can be treated in this way and it is a joy for people who have to move house frequently to be able to take cherished specimens with them.

A pergola gives dappled shade with an airy feel to it, the space within enclosed lightly. The structure should be distinguished enough to stand on its own merits in winter; in summer, swathed with wisteria, jasmine, grapevines, roses, honeysuckles and clematis, it makes a magical place to sit, screened from the world beyond. It may be free-standing, or fixed to the side of the house or to a high garden wall.

'Pleached bowers where honeysuckles, ripened by the sun, forbid the sun to enter' ... in a smaller garden, bowers and arbours will provide enough shade for a bench seat and perhaps a small table; drape them with the same plants as for pergolas and tunnels, choosing the less vigorous varieties.

The smaller the garden, the more important the use of all walls and fences, but sunny walls are the most valuable. Make the beds as wide as possible and plant well away from the wall, at about twelve to eighteen inches (30–45cm), so that the plants can get all the available moisture. Soil at the foot of a wall is often impoverished and full of rubble, but once it has been cleared and enriched

In this bright corner of a Los Angeles courtyard, dark blue pots, exotic foliage and colourful flowers make it an enchanting place in which to relax or dine. (DESIGNER Mel Light)

Roses, jasmine, solanum, variegated Viburnum tinus *and the glaucous-leaved* Melianthus major *are amongst the plants tangling so gloriously in this small back garden.* (DESIGNER Thomasina Tarling)

many plants do very well there. With a strip-garden, those few narrow inches between house and road or pavement (sidewalk), this improvement of the soil is even more vital to success. Remove what earth there is, excavate the beds or planting holes and enlarge as far as possible. Break up the subsoil, add some organic material to enrich the sifted soil and return it. If excavation is not possible and the soil is shallow, it may be possible to build up a low bed there, as long as the top of it is kept well below the damp-proof course. Alternatively, use deep but narrow planters, made to measure if necessary, from wood, brick or concrete. With such thorough preparation, climbers (vines) and wall-plants should thrive there, smaller shrubs, perennials and annuals clustering about their feet. Using wire, trellis, wall-nails and vine-eyes, the plants can be trained over the walls to make an arresting picture.

A porch or protective canopy above a door will support a flower-filled trough; tubs and pots at each side of the door and up the steps, windowboxes and even my pet abominations, hanging baskets, all will make the most here of what little space there is. Even wall-trained grape-vines and fruit trees are a possibility, herbs and vegetables too, but whether the dust and likely pollution in such a situation makes this sensible is debatable. Whatever is grown here, regular feeding and watering plus a weekly hose-down will help to keep the plants happy and healthy.

Climbers (vines) of all kinds are always the small-garden owner's best friends, for despite their abundant charms they take up so little ground space. Train the more vigorous creatures on galvanized wires stretched tightly between vine-eyes hammered or screwed into the walls. String the first wire about two or three feet (60–90cm) above the ground, the rest at intervals of about two feet (60cm). To avoid the rather unattractive look of the bare wires, add the strands gradually as the plants grow.

Less rampageous wall-plants and annual climbers (vines) are often tied directly to wall-nails as they grow. Trellis panels are also excellent for these plants: choose sturdy wood, as flimsy trellis does not last, unless using trellis purely decoratively rather than as a plant support, when something lightweight is perfectly adequate. If the architecture of the house allows, a well-made trellis covering virtually the whole wall is an ornament in its own right, a useful plant-support and an excellent disguise for an imperfect wall; it also allows a surprising number of plants to be grown in a very small garden.

When training fruit on the walls (apples, apricots, cherries, figs, peaches, plums, nectarines, etc.) get them into place before anything else, to ensure them enough room; they hate to be jostled. It takes a bit of skill to grow and train them well; I recommend studying a book that instructs in the art.

After that, the first choice must surely be wisteria, which loves sun and a well-manured soil; once it gets its toes in, the growth is phenomenal, reaching up to the roof before long. One must be able to cope with climbing an undulating ladder twice a year in order to tie in the new growth and give the necessary pruning. Without this treatment wisteria is unlikely to flower well and will become a monster that wraps itself around everything in sight. There are many varieties, all bearing long racemes of scented flowers in various shades of mauve, purple and white, and the foliage remains attractive when the flowers die. A plant may take a year or two before deciding to flower, but *W. sinensis* 'Prematura' and 'Prematura Alba' are said to be a little more eager.

'Ah, these jasmines, these white jasmines, I seem to remember when I first filled my hands with these white jasmines, these white jasmines ...' wrote the Indian poet Rabindranath Tagore, and they have always been an essential ingredient of gardens, loved because of their romantic appearance and fragrance. There are several to choose from: *Jasminum officinale* is the familiar white-flowered summer jasmine, the hardiest of the bunch, scented, vigorous and ubiquitous, but none the worse for that. There is also a variegated form, 'Argenteovariegatum', and another with yellow leaves. More tender are the pink-flowered *J. beesianum* and *J.* x *stephanense*, while only in a particularly warm and sheltered place is it worth trying the lovely evergreens, double yellow *J. mesnyi* (*J. primulinum*), and

J. polyanthum, which has the most richly scented white flowers. To increase their chances of survival in colder areas, these and similarly tender things should be given a winter overcoat of straw, bracken or dead leaves, kept in place by netting or sheets of spun polyester (Reemay). There is one other member of the family to be warmly recommended, *Jasminum humile* 'Revolutum', an evergreen wall shrub that in summer has small, sweetly scented yellow flowers.

Room must be found for at least one climbing rose, surely. Almost all roses do better in the sun except where it is truly fierce. Those varieties that also flower well in shade, I use there, keeping the warmest walls for the more rarefied creatures, such as the double yellow Banksian rose, *Rosa banksiae* 'Lutea', which is faintly but deliciously scented. While the magnificent yellow 'Mermaid' is tolerant of shade in warm areas, in colder places it needs a sunny, sheltered place to succeed.

'Climbing Cécile Brunner' is an entrancing, fragrant thing, reaching to some twenty feet (6m), and smothered by small, clear-pink roses of a delicate shape at midsummer, with occasional flowers after that. Another lovely climber, the sweetly scented 'Phyllis Bide', has yellow flowers that are flushed with salmon (which sounds absolutely beastly, like 'Masquerade', but do not be put off, for they are charming) borne over several months and will climb to twelve feet (3.5m) or more. While many roses are widely distributed across the world, there are always a few good ones that for some reason or other remain largely unknown outside their own country and these are worth searching for. Most countries have a rose society, and indeed many other specialist groups, which are good sources of information and advice. In some parts, notably areas of North America, roses are often cut right down to ground level in severe winters, but the toughest ones will survive and shoot up again in spring, especially if they are earthed up and given a protective jacket of some kind.

PLANTS FOR SUN

Grow borderline plants against a sunny wall, or in open ground in favoured areas

TREES AND TREE-LIKE SHRUBS
Acacia Z8
Azara Z8
Ceanothus Z9
Cytisus battandieri Z7
Fremontodendron
Magnolia (evergreen) Z6

SHRUBS
Abelia Z5
Abutilon Z5
Aloysia triphylla Z8
Brachyglottis
Buddleja, to Z5
Ceanothus Z9
Choisya Z7
Cistus Z7
Corokia Z8
Embothrium Z8
Escallonia Z8

Hebe, to Z6
Helichrysum
Leptospermum Z9
Myrtus Z8
Phlomis
Phygelia capensis Z8
Prunus triloba Z5
Punica Z9
Rhaphiolepis Z8

CLIMBERS AND WALL SHRUBS
Campsis, to Z4
Clematis (many)
Clianthus Z8
Cobaea scandens Z9
Convolvulus tricolor 'Heavenly Blue' Z8
Eccremocarpus Z9
Hoheria Z8
Jasminum mesnyi Z8
J. officinale Z7
J. polyanthum Z8
J. 'Revolutum' Z8
Lapageria rosea Z9

Leptospermum Z9
Passiflora caerulea Z7
P. c. 'Constance Elliott' Z7
Plumbago auriculata Z9
Rhodochiton Z9
Solanum crispum 'Glasnevin' Z8
S. jasminoides 'Album' Z9
Sollya heterophylla Z9
Trachelospermum asiaticum Z9
T. jasminoides Z9
Tropaeolum speciosum Z8
T. j. 'Variegatum'

ANNUALS
Amaranthus
Antirrhinum
Alcea
Bellis perennis
Bidens
Brachycome
Brassica
Campanula
Convolvulus
Cosmos

Dianthus
Dimorphotheca/Osteospermum
Felicia
Gypsophila
Lathyrus odoratus
Lavatera
Limnanthes
Lobelia
Matthiola
Nigella
Onopordum
Papaver
Pelargonium
Petunia
Phlox
Ricinus
Rudbeckia
Salvia
Senecio cineraria
Tropaeolum
Verbena
Viola

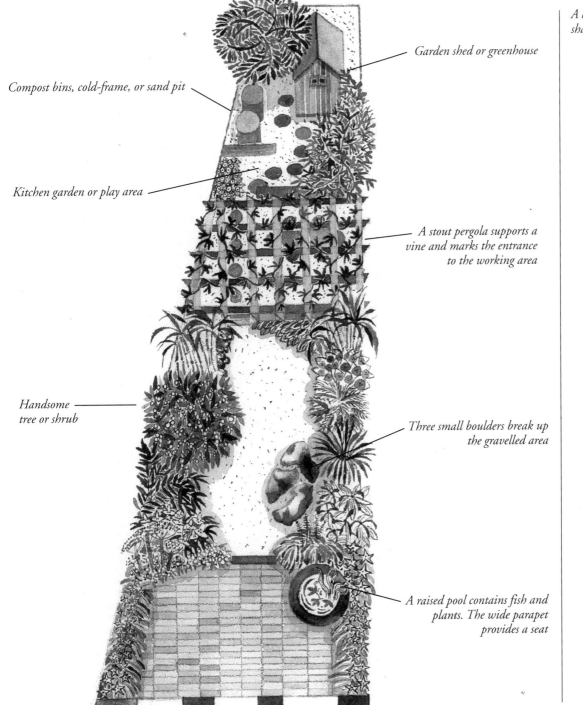

A design for a wedge-shaped plot.

Garden shed or greenhouse

Compost bins, cold-frame, or sand pit

Kitchen garden or play area

A stout pergola supports a vine and marks the entrance to the working area

Handsome tree or shrub

Three small boulders break up the gravelled area

A raised pool contains fish and plants. The wide parapet provides a seat

GREY, GLAUCOUS AND SILVER-TONED PLANTS

(Most prefer sun and well-drained soils)

TREES AND TREE-LIKE SHRUBS
Chamaecyparis 'Boulevard' Z6
Cytisus battandieri Z8
Elaeagnus angustifolia Z2
Eucalyptus gunnii Z8
Pyrus salicifolia 'Pendula' Z4
Salix exigua Z2
Sorbus hupehensis Z6

SHRUBS
Artemisia, to Z4
Atriplex Z8
Brachyglottis 'Sunshine'
Buddleja crispa Z8
B. fallowiana Z8
B. 'Lochinch' Z8
Caryopteris x clandonensis Z7
Cistus 'Silver Pink' Z8
C. x skanbergii Z8
Convolvulus cneorum Z8
Corokia Z8

Euonymus fortunei 'Silver Queen' Z5
Halimium Z8
Hebe albicans Z8
H. pimeloides Z7
H. pinguifolia Z6
H. p. 'Pagei' Z6
H. 'Pewter Dome' Z8
Helianthemum (some) to Z5
Helichrysum italicum Z8
H. petiolare Z10
Hippophae rhamnoides Z3
Lavandula, several, to Z5
Melianthus major Z8
Olearia Z8
Ozothamnus rosmarinifolius Z8
Perovskia Z5
Phlomis Z7
Potentilla, some, to Z5
Romneya Z7
Rosa glauca Z2
Rosmarinus Z6
Ruta Z5
Santolina Z7

Teucrium fruticans Z8
Yucca whipplei Z8

CLIMBERS
Coronilla glauca Z9
C. g. 'Variegata' Z9
Lonicera (several, inc. *L. x heckrottii* Z5)

PERENNIALS
Acaena Z6
Acanthus, some, to Z6
Achillea, to Z2
Anaphalis Z3
Anthemis tinctoria Z6
Artemisia, to Z4
Astelia Z9
Aurinia saxatilis Z3
Ballota Z8
Cerastium tomentosum Z4
Crambe Z6
Cynara Z6
Dianthus, some, to Z3
Dicentra, some, to Z5

Echinops Z3
Eryngium, to Z5
Hosta (some)
Lamium maculatum, several, inc. 'Beacon Silver' Z4
Lychnis coronaria cvs. Z4
Onopordum Z6
Pulmonaria, several, to Z3
Romneya Z7
Salvia argentea Z5
Senecio cineraria, Z8
Stachys byzantina Z5
Tanacetum, several, to Z5
Thymus citriodorus 'Silver Queen' Z7

GRASSES
Cortaderia selloana 'Pumila' Z5
Festuca glauca Z5
Helictotrichon sempervirens Z4

ANNUALS AND BIENNIALS
Papaver (some), to Z3
Verbascum, many, to Z5

I long to plant all those roses described by Graham Stuart Thomas in *Climbing Roses, Old and New* as needing the shelter of a warm wall in Surrey – an evocative phrase conjuring up ancient sports cars and cries of 'Sorry, partner!' floating across the tennis lawns. The names are enticing: who were those delicate beauties, 'Aimée Vibert', 'Céline Forestier', 'Belle Portugaise', 'La Follette', 'Madame Sancy de Parabère', peachy 'Lady Hillingdon' and the rest? No doubt they flourish without such a sheltered wall in warmer parts of the world.

For small gardens there are several roses that will reach to about eight feet (2.5m) or a little more. My favourite, 'Aloha', has old-fashioned blooms of a beautiful pink and the old tea-rose fragrance. Other good ones are 'Dream Girl', 'Parade', 'Picture', 'Pink Perpetué', 'Pompon de Paris', 'Ritter von Barmstede' (all pink); 'Schoolgirl' (a delicious burnt apricot); 'Guinée' and 'Ena Harkness' (both deeply red and richly perfumed); 'Golden Showers' and 'Casino' (yellow); 'Handel' (white, touched with pink); 'Purity', 'White Cockade' and 'Climbing Iceberg' (all white). These may also be grown on walls and fences around the rest of the garden and on poles, pillars or obelisks in the borders.

Clematis are the ideal companions for roses and many other wall-shrubs, twining their way among them very decoratively. Most will grow on a south or west wall as long as they are given a moisture-retentive soil and their roots are shaded by other plants and an old tile. Choose them so that their colours enhance that of their hosts or extend the seasonal interest by flowering before and after the roses bloom; as there is a clematis in bloom during every month of the year, this strategy is easy enough to achieve. The most vigorous clematis, such as the montanas, are best grown in some isolation, nipping up to the eaves, sprawling over a wall or strong trellis (it will *need* to be strong),

The unusual, pink and white 'paint-splashed' leaves of Actinidia kolomikta.

smothering an outhouse or oil-tank and flaunting themselves from the top of a tree.

New large-flowered hybrid clematis appear every year; not all stand the test of time and many old ones are still the best. Where there is trouble in establishing some of the large-flowered clematis or where they suffer from wilt, often the smaller-flowered ones will thrive. In town or country, I have had very little trouble with varieties of *C. alpina, armandii, cirrhosa, macropetala, montana, texensis, viticella* and others; all are enchanting and some are scented, more than can be said for their flamboyant relatives. Clematis are just as delightful grown on fences, trellis, walls, shrubs, trees, arches, arbours, pillars and poles. They make good ground cover and, like most flexible climbers (vines), will fall happily, cascading over banks and retaining walls.

Actinidias are attractive, with heart-shaped leaves, small flowers and, in warm climates, edible fruit: the green leaves of *Actinidia kolomikta* are dashingly splashed with pink and white. Other good wall plants include campsis, the everlasting pea (*Lathyrus latifolius),* solanums, the evergreens *Pileostegia viburnoides, Stauntonia hexaphylla* and *Trachelospermum jasminoides*, also many grape-vines, including *Vitis* 'Brant' and purple-leaved *Vitis vinifera* 'Purpurea', while the magnificently ornamental, large-leaved *Vitis coignetiae* colours up dramatically in the autumn (fall).

Below and between the climbers (vines), covering any straggly bare stems, there are so many useful shrubs to be grown on a warm wall or fence that I shall only mention a few favourites here. The blue-flowered, evergreen ceanothus or Californian lilacs are invaluable; quick-growing *C. rigidus* is one of the earliest, but all have their charms and one or other of them will be in flower from spring to autumn.

Abelia floribunda and *A.* x *grandiflora* are two beautiful plants; the first has rosy flowers, while those of the latter are pink and white, and scented; *A.* x *g.* 'Francis Mason' is particularly good. If you want something brighter, either the bright yellow flowers of the semi-evergreen *Fremontodendron californicum* or the nodding, red-and-yellow flowers of *Abutilon megapotamicum* could be just the note. *Choisya ternata*, the Mexican orange blossom, is a useful evergreen with scented white flowers. Escallonias, also evergreen, with small flowers of either pink, white or red, are other good plants here.

One of the bonuses of many cistus is their aromatic foliage, sweetly spicy in hot sun. The leaves are either green or silver, and the delicate flowers are white, pink or shades of pink and pinkish purple, often with a conspicuous basal blotch: *C. x hybridus* and *C. ladanifer* are especially charming.

Convolvulus cneorum is a pet, about two feet (60cm) high and wide, with the most delightful little white flowers just blushed with pink, the foliage remaining a shimmering silver mound all year; it seems happy on chalk or limestone. I would also want to try lemon verbena (*Aloysia triphylla*), the sweetly scented *Daphne odora* 'Aureomarginata', hebes, hydrangeas and myrtle. Equally good are many of the small grey-leaved things: artemisias, rock-roses, the curry plant (*Helichrysum italicum*), senecio (now called *Brachyglottis* 'Sunshine'), ozothamnus, cotton lavender (*Santolina chamaecyparissus*), *Teucrium fruticans,* and the dear, familiar herbs lavender, rosemary, thyme and, not least, sage in all its grey-green, gold and purple forms.

Many of the plants mentioned here will also do well in the other parts of a sunny garden and somewhere room must be found for a buddleia (if only for the sake of the butterflies), preferably the desirable *Buddleja* 'Lochinch', which has soft grey leaves and fragrant lavender flowers, or *B. davidii* 'Harlequin', also fragrant, with variegated leaves and purple flowers; both these should be cut down almost to the ground in early spring. Even more to be prized, *B. alternifolia* can be grown as a standard, and then weeps charmingly like a small lilac fountain; it is scented and can be trimmed back lightly after flowering. A rather unusual shrub or small tree for a sunny, well-drained place, the Japanese bitter-orange, *Poncirus trifoliata*, has dark green, deciduous leaves, sharp spines, fragrant white blossom and small, orange-like fruit.

Many lilacs will grow too large and sucker too freely to be ideal, while their dead flower heads

An unusual copper arch and a curving pathway, inset with blue tiles, contribute much to the charm of this well-planted garden in San Francisco. (DESIGNER Keeyla Meadows)

The outsize clump of bamboo, the large, striking sculpture and the wall panel of Roman mosiac behind it all have drastic impact in this outstanding little garden. (DESIGNER Michael Nicholson)

look ugly for months, but *Syringa* x *persica* will behave beautifully, remaining neat and covered in late spring by scented lilac flowers. *Pyrus salicifolia* 'Pendula' is a pretty thing, weeping like a little silver willow; at about ten feet (3m) high and wide, it will fit into almost any garden and looks well with small-flowered roses like 'Ballerina', 'Yesterday' and 'Nozomi'.

As virtually all bush roses will thrive in sun (if it is not too violent), there is no point in making a long list, for the choice is an individual thing, depending much on personal taste and the planting scheme, although the brighter, more fiercely coloured varieties are likely to have a disruptive effect in a small garden. The larger, more rampant growers will not be suitable, while hybrid teas are too gawky and tend not to do well in the scrum of a mixed border, but most cluster-flowered and smaller shrub roses should be perfectly happy. Those that have single flowers or an old-fashioned look seem particularly at home among other shrubs: 'Dainty Maid', 'Golden Wings' and 'Lavender Lassie' are excellent, but many with a long flowering period and some scent will do.

In my last garden, which was some twenty feet by seventy (6 x 21m), divided up into three more-or-less equal sections, I grew a few old-fashioned-looking roses – 'Boule de Neige', tall and erect, her creamy-white flowers crimson in the bud; 'Louise Odier', flowering away for most of the summer and pushing through anything in her way so that one was constantly surprised as her tightly packed pink flower-heads burst out where least expected, most charmingly through a *Cotinus* 'Royal Purple'. Shell-like 'Madame Pierre Oger' has ivory flowers, blushed with rose in sunny weather. Thornless 'Zéphirine Drouhin', with large, scented flowers of cerise pink, is rather *outrée* but very charming, like a Gaiety Girl, though sadly susceptible to mildew in many gardens, including mine. Then 'Reine des Violettes', with grey-green foliage and the most beautifully shaped flowers of a warm ash-purple (a description that does no justice to its charms), and 'Buff Beauty', one of the loveliest, I think, with tea-scented, soft apricot flowers and an arching form. I also had 'Cornelia' with her *frisettes* of burnt apricot fading to creamy pink, and 'Felicia', also apricot-pink and very free-flowering. I longed for many others of these lovely things which were so generous and trouble-free.

The smallest garden could accommodate at least one small rose or even a group of three. Best of all here, I think, is pink-flowered 'Nathalie Nypels'. ('How names can kill,' remarked Brigadier Lucas Phillips, who first drew her to my attention, in *Roses for Small Gardens*; little did he know that the Powers that Be have now dubbed her 'Mevrouw Nathalie Nypels'.) But apart from that, she has all the virtues, being a neat three feet high and wide (90 x 90cm), healthy, seldom out of flower, and well-scented. 'Yvonne Rabier' is equally charming (and the name is an improvement), much the same size, with glossy leaves and small, double white flowers that have just a hint of lemon to them. I am not sure that calling a rose 'The Fairy' is much of a help to it, but what a useful little rose this is, about two feet by a spreading four (60 x 120cm), absolutely covered with pink button-flowers, very good for ground cover or splashing over a low wall, flowering from just after midsummer until Christmas. 'White Pet' is as engaging as the name suggests, even smaller than the others, and bearing its tiny, pompon-like flowers throughout the summer. All these can be grown among other small shrubs, or in beds edged with low-clipped evergreens, but there I like to underplant them with silver foliage or low-growing campanulas, pansies, alpine strawberries, annuals and so on.

Most herbaceous perennials enjoy the sun: a few to choose from, all reasonably easy, might include tall, handsome-leaved *Acanthus mollis* and *Acanthus spinosus*, *Achillea* 'Moonshine', which has soft, yellow, plate-like flower heads, the Michaelmas daisy *Aster* x *frikartii*, low-growing, pale-yellow alyssum (*Aurinia saxatilis* var. 'Citrina'), lavender-flowered nepeta, tall, sword-leaved *Crocosmia* 'Lucifer', a few fleshy euphorbias, the stunning cranesbills *Geranium psilostemon* and *G.* 'Johnson's Blue', irises, the small, yellow-flowered hot poker *Kniphofia* 'Little Maid', the great silver thistle *Onopordon acanthium*, one or two peonies, oriental poppies, especially 'Perry's White', purple-flowered *Salvia* x *superba,* the ice-plants *Sedum spectabile* and *Sedum* 'Herbstfreude' (syn. 'Autumn Joy'), both good for the butterflies, the variegated sisyrinchium 'Aunt May', some ornamental grasses ... where to stop? I could go on and on, yet still leave out many indispensable plants, and then there are the biennials, annuals and bulbs ...

As for water, here there may be pools, wall-fountains, canals, either moving or still, although the sound of moving water is particularly welcome in the sun. Perhaps best of all is a sunken pool, the water lying just below the paving, when all the reflections of the sky and the surrounding plants are laid out before us: for this, the larger the pool, the better. The water can be left as a mirror or planted with waterlilies, marginal plants and oxygenators, the goldfish moving constantly between them in that mysterious way they have. Both waterlilies and fish like a sunny pool, but the latter need some shade as well. This is usually provided by the lily-pads, but a shelter made from a length of drain-pipe or a slate, supported on bricks, is better, giving them somewhere to hide when predators are about. About two-thirds of the pool should be left unplanted as it is the contrast between the plants and the plain stretches of water that is so effective. Neither goldfish nor lilies enjoy turbulent water and lilies hate a splashing, so if there is a fountain let it be a small, bubbling thing: this the fish do enjoy, or mine do, becoming childishly frolicsome when it is switched on. With luck, frogs, toads and occasionally newts will arrive in a well-stocked pool. Birds, hoverflies and dragonflies are also drawn to water. Fortunately there are several small-to-miniature waterlilies that grow in a few inches of water and are ideal for little ponds and container pools. There are also restrained water-plants and miniature rushes that will look well there. All may be planted directly into the soil at the bottom and margins of the pond or, more usually these days, in plastic baskets of an appropriate size, using an aquatic soil mix; this helps to keep the plants under control and maintenance easy.

Where there is really no room for even a small pool, place shallow bowls brimming with water to reflect the sky. I have an old marble mortar here, about fourteen inches (35cm) high and wide, where leaves and petals drift on the water like the tiniest of waterlilies (when they do not arrive there naturally, I cheat). The birds adore it: I have counted fourteen of them perched on its side, dipping and bobbing away in happy frenzy. Beside it is the shallower dish they use as a splash-bath.

At the other end of the scale, I have seen a sunny backyard where almost the entire surface area was under water, apart from some planting, mainly bamboo, around the boundaries, a timber deck outside the house and a small pavilion on a little island at the far end, reached by stepping stones. There were water-plants, fish, even a couple of ducks. It had great charm but would not do for small children or dogs (though no doubt cats would enjoy the fish).

As to a kitchen garden, apart from a few herbs, I cannot bear to spare much precious space in a small garden for vegetables. In addition to the risk of their being dangerously polluted in an urban garden, there are too many other things I want to cram in, but if a small garden is long enough and gets enough sun, one section could be set aside for herbs, fruit and vegetables. One might lay out a potager (edible landscape) in full view, but the conventional vegetable plot is best hidden at the far end of the site. The alternative is to grow a few things in the borders or in containers. Herbs and most saladings do well, runner beans will clamber up the trellis and grape-vines drape the pergola. Drop in such things as standard gooseberries, clumps of rhubarb, ruby chard and other odds and ends wherever there is a suitable space and remember that alpine strawberries, chives, parsley, sage and thyme make good edging-plants.

But in the main, we are here for the sun, the scent and the flowers...

> *Soon will the high midsummer pomps come on,*
> *Soon will the musk carnations brake and swell,*
> *Soon shall we have the gold-dusted snapdragon,*
> *Sweet William with his homely cottage smell,*
> *And stocks in fragrant blow;*
> *Roses that down the alley shine afar,*
> *And open, jasmine-muffled lattices*
> *And groups under the dreaming garden trees*
> *And the full moon, and the white evening star.*

MATTHEW ARNOLD (1822–88)

6

O BLESSED SHADES,
O GENTLE COOL RETREAT

The Shaded Garden

Happy retreat, who would not but be made
The joyful tenant of so blest a shade?
Who higher could their fond ambition trace
Than in the enjoyment of so sweet a place?
Here undisturbed within these shades to rove
Nor envy gods their famed Idalian Grove.

A. MERRICK OF AYLESBURY (EIGHTEENTH CENTURY)

OPPOSITE: *Masterly restraint is shown in this formal garden. Clipped ivy surrounds the circular pool and fountain with just a few white flowers allowed. In the background, a charmingly supercilious crane peers out of the gloom. (Lord Snowdon's London garden)*

HONEYSUCKLE, CLEMATIS, JASMINE AND ROSES lie swathed across the white walls and the dusky-blue trellis: languorous, loud with bees, and scenting the air. Not in some sun-warmed corner, as you might expect, but jostling comfortably on the coolest wall of a shaded city plot. Such unexpected pleasures are among the many bonuses of town gardens; the slightly higher air temperature found there, together with the shelter and residual warmth of even the shaded walls, makes all sorts of delightful and surprising things possible.

In hot countries, how we crave a little shade – yet in colder climates many of us shrink from the very idea of a shaded garden. Nevertheless, the owners of such gardens know that their bleak reputation is not deserved. True, the middle gardens of a row of houses that face away from the sun may go a little short of the brightest light, but some light there will be, and where shade is inevitable, it should be treated as an ally and a friend. While the charm of such a garden is particularly welcome in hot weather, all year round it should remain distinguished, in an agreeably understated way.

Apart from this, those parts of a garden that avoid the early-morning sun are valuable in cold areas for growing plants such as camellias which resent being thawed out too quickly after frost; other plants – honeysuckles, Japanese maples and many clematis, for instance – will find life more tolerable if sheltered at midday from the fierce sun overhead.

The all-green garden is not to be despised; there are plants of so many shapes, so many shades and textures of green, that such a garden need never be dull and its simplicity is often welcome.

A gob-smacked bronze fish dribbles water into a pebble-filled pool, making it a safe water feature if small children are about. (DESIGNER Jill Billington)

Nevertheless, colour and some light, or at least an impression of these, can be brought in if we so wish.

When the house and garden walls are white or pastel-coloured, everything at once seems brighter, while deep pinks and rosy terracottas make a warm backdrop, especially for evergreen shrubs and those exotic-looking creatures that drape themselves about so generously, twining along wires, up drain-pipes and along any support that is offered to them. Actinidias, for instance, with their vigorous tendrils, heart-shaped leaves and creamy-white flowers, or the bright coral plant (*Berberidopsis corallina*) and the lovely, scented *Clematis armandii* which, although recommended for full sun, thrives on sheltered, shaded walls in temperate climate zones, its paddle-shaped evergreen leaves still handsome when the smothering of white flowers has gone.

Apart from the walls, the paintwork used in the garden, on doors, trellis, furniture, etc., together with the statues and other ornaments, will also help dispel the gloom. White or pale blue furniture, marble statues, gleaming metal sculpture, glass spheres, all these work well. Mirrors are useful: whether set in an arch, behind a wrought-iron gate, in false windows, behind trellis, or edged by clipped shrubs and ivy, they reflect a considerable amount of light into the garden. Even a small mirror, hung like a plaque on a wall, brings a little sparkle. (The windows of neighbouring houses may also do this, but that is a factor beyond our control.)

Although a shaded terrace may not get quite so much use as a sunny one, it should still be a generous size whenever possible, for it is a good place to relax or to entertain on hot days. The flooring choices here include slabs of all kinds, tiles, pavers, bricks and granite setts, or combinations of some of these, together with pebbles and cobbles. Marble is fine for shade in hot countries but looks dispiriting in cool ones. Gravel is truly excellent, for it does not become slippery as bricks and slabs tend to do in areas of high rainfall (although they can be kept clear with a stiff brush and patent stone-cleaners). Timber, decking in particular, makes a good foil for those architectural evergreen plants that grow so well in shaded areas – fatsia, mahonia, bamboo, bergenia, pachysandra, etc. – but one must think twice before using it in damp climates, where it can become slippery.

Grass seldom succeeds in shade, even when sown from the recommended seed mixtures, while the plants often suggested as substitutes for grass seldom do well in areas that receive much wear. For a purely visual effect, tough, glossy-leaved ivy is excellent and will repay some nurturing with good soil, feeding and regular clipping. Low-growing, evergreen *Pachysandra terminalis* and its variegated form are particularly good in acid soils. Box or boxwood (*Buxus sempervirens*) planted in squares or rectangles and shorn to a few inches high makes satisfying slabs of low-level greenery in light shade. In a small, damp area, plants such as the tiny-leaved Corsican mint (*Mentha requienii*) and mind-your-own-business (*Soleirolia soleirolii*) are perfect, while a moss lawn has much quiet charm. In hot regions, the star jasmine (*Trachelospermum jasminoides*), normally a sun-loving climber, can be grown as ground cover in light shade.

Water is as desirable in the shade as it is in the sun, but has different character there. In sun it is a lively thing, each ripple catching the light, every splashing drop a prism. In shade it takes on a still, contemplative quality and yet there is a cool, sinuous and green feel to it which is deliciously

PLANTS FOR DEGREES OF SHADE

SHRUBS
Aucuba Z7
Bamboos
Berberis, to Z5
Buxus Z7
Camellia Z7
Chaenomeles
Choisya Z7
Elaeagnus Z7
Euonymus, to Z5
Fatsia Z8
Fuchsia, to Z6
Garrya Z8
Gaultheria Z4
Hydrangea Z5
Ilex, to Z5
Kalmia Z4
Ligustrum Z7
Lonicera pileata Z5
Mahonia, to Z5
Osmanthus, to Z6
Pachysandra terminalis Z5
Philadelphus coronarius 'Aurea' Z5
Pieris, to Z5
Prunus laurocerasus Z7

Rhododendron
Sarcococca Z6
Skimmia Z7
Viburnum tinus Z7
Vinca, to Z4

CLIMBERS
Actinidia, to Z4
Akebia Z5
Berberidopsis Z8
Celastrus, to Z2
Clematis (many)
Fallopia baldschuanica
Hedera (most)
Humulus lupulus Z5
Hydrangea anomala Z5
Jasminum nudiflorum Z6
J. officinale Z7
Lapageria Z9
Lonicera (many), to Z4
Parthenocissus henryana Z7
P. quinquefolia Z3
P. tricuspidata Z4
Schizophragma hydrangeoides Z5
Vitis coignetiae

PERENNIALS
Alchemilla
Anemone x hybrida cvs. Z6
Aquilegia vulgaris Z4
Aruncus Z7
Astrantia Z6
Bergenia, to Z3
Brunnera Z3
Campanula, to Z3
Cimicifuga, to Z4
Convallaria Z3
Digitalis
Epimedium Z5
Ferns (most)
Geranium (some), to Z5
Helleborus Z6
Hemerocallis, to Z4
Heuchera, to Z3
Heucherella, Z5
Hosta
Iris foetidissima
Lamium Z4
Liriope Z6
Luzula Z6
Milium effusum 'Aureum' Z6

Polygonum affine Z3
Primula
Pulmonaria, to Z3
Saxifraga (some)
Soleirolia
Symphytum Z5
Tellima Z6
Tiarella Z3
Tolmiea menziesii Z7
Trillium Z5

ANNUALS AND BIENNIALS
Begonia x carrierei flore-pleno
   (semperflorens)
Begonia rex
Bidens
Collinsia heterophylla
Digitalis
Fuchsia
Impatiens
Lunaria
Mimulus
Myosotis
Nicotiana
(many others will take some shade)

sinister. The smallest shaded pool or shallow bowl, set among ferns and hostas, has as much charm in its quiet way as the grandest lily-pond; a wall-fountain trickling over gleaming stones is as entrancing as any cascading set-piece. One such I know, on the wall of an old house, receives no sunlight at all, but water spouts from the dolphin's mouth into a mossy clam-shell and from there it drips and splashes down to the cobblestones below, misting the ferns and ivies, delightful on hot days and elegantly melancholic beneath an overcast sky. However, if there should be some sun in one part of the garden, a pool there reflects useful light back into the shade; nothing is more pleasing than to lie in bed and watch the reflections from a near-by pool rippling across the ceiling.

Many plants flourish in shade if the soil has been prepared thoroughly. It is always worth taking a risk or two with something we long to grow, even if it is not particularly recommended for shade. It may sulk, in which case sling it elsewhere, but could do very well, giving that particular pleasure which comes from confounding the experts.

Some of the loveliest plants, including camellias, hydrangeas and rhododendrons, will do well here, as will many roses, clematis and honeysuckles. Others, such as aucubas, ferns, ivies, etc., tolerate a positively Stygian gloom. Plants with gold, silver or variegated leaves are particularly cheering in a gloomy spot. While some yellow foliage turns green in the shade, others, like the golden robinia almost too bright in full sun – take on a subtle glow in dappled shade; like a catalpa, this robinia can be kept small, cut down almost to ground level in spring, the leaves becoming even larger.

The yellow-leaved mock orange, *Philadelphus coronarius* 'Aureus', prefers shade; it scorches in full sun (the white, scented flowers are a bonus). Those evergreen elaeagnus with gold variations,

Cherubs embrace atop an ivy-covered wall, apparently oblivious to the snarling god below them, who is almost obscured by the surrounding foliage.

such as *Elaeagnus pungens* 'Maculata' or *E.* x *ebbingei* 'Gilt Edge', gleam on through the depths of winter. Its columnar shape and polished leaves make *Euonymus japonicus* 'Président Gauthier' a shining pillar which is very effective, either on its own or at the centre of a group of lower, more rounded plants. On a smaller scale, both the acid-yellow bamboo *Pleioblastus viridistriatus* and Bowles' golden grass glow away cheerfully in dim corners.

For a touch of silver, *Rhamnus alaternus* 'Argenteovariegata' is outstanding, while in a smaller garden, *Euonymus fortunei* 'Silver Queen', with an eventual height and spread of about six feet (1.8m), is as good as its name suggests. Another useful privet, *Ligustrum sinense* 'Variegatum', is resilient but refined; with grey-green white-edged leaves, the impression is silvery. It grows to a medium height and is excellent in shade. A friend planted a pair of them in the darkest part of her garden, one on each side of a small statue in front of a trellised mirror, and all these have turned it into a delicately bosky corner.

As to white roses, 'Boule de Neige' flowers very well, 'Iceberg' too, and 'Margaret Merril', with hints of spice in her white flowers. If there is room, the rugosa 'Blanc Double de Coubert' is superb and not picky about soil; five feet by four (1.5 x 1.2m), with white, semi-double flowers that have a delectable scent and bright hips in autumn.

The warm, sheltered beds by the house walls are particularly useful in the shade. While most climbing roses will produce some flowers here, some are more generous than others. Above all, 'Mrs Herbert Stevens', a darling, has deliciously scented white flowers, and despite a delicate air, puts up with poor soil as well as shade. 'Mermaid' is a glad-handed rose wherever one puts her; excellent for a shaded, cool wall in warm or sheltered areas, and though supposed to need a sunny wall elsewhere, I have seen an old specimen looking magnificent against a chilly wall in the north of England. 'Gloire de Dijon' is a gloriously scented good-doer of quite a different yellow – buff, with hints of apricot-pink in it. 'Madame Alfred Carrière' is equally obliging, producing a succession of fragrant, globular white flowers of great charm.

There must surely be a red rose. Graham Stuart Thomas, in *Climbing Roses, Old and New,* recommends 'Souvenir de Claudius Denoyel' and it is irresistible: scented crimson flowers borne in a tremendous flush at midsummer, and some thereafter. Free-flowering 'Parkdirektor Riggers' is also wonderfully crimson and slightly scented, but oh, what a name for a lovely rose. One hopes the fortunate *parkdirektor* deserved such a tribute. Pretty, pink 'Bantry Bay' is seldom suggested for gloom, but two grew in terracotta pots outside my kitchen door for eight years, covered with blooms all summer, despite getting only an hour of evening sun. I took them with me on leaving, stuffed into a plastic pot, where they suffered six months of neglect. Then, planted out in an east-facing bed, one turned up its toes after a year, but the other goes from strength to strength.

Flowering once, in early summer, 'Madame Grégoire Staechlin' is a stunner who should be given a place in any but the tiniest garden; with a sweet-pea fragrance, the large, semi-double flowers of warm pink are strung gloriously along her branches, followed in the autumn by flame-coloured hips which last for months. Glossy-leaved 'New Dawn' produces her delicate, shell-pink blooms a little later in the summer, then flowers throughout the season; both grow to about twenty feet (6m).

Here I have the pleasure of them dropping in from my neighbours' gardens. If one is fortunate enough to possess gardening neighbours, one can arrange things so that those on each side plant some different, ravishing thing while we, piggy-in-the-middle, provide yet another, to the mutual benefit of all. This friendly practice make the best possible use of small gardens.

Several clematis flower well on a north or east wall. I love best those with white flowers: 'Marie Boisselot' (syn. 'Mme Le Coultre') is a wonder, and the strange double, greenish-white 'Duchess of Edinburgh' always intrigues. Here I have also the deliciously blue 'Perle d'Azur' entwined with a 'Mermaid' rose. All these get but a brief glimpse of the morning sun, and another in the evening, but undeterred, flower away bravely. Pink 'Comtesse de Bouchaud' (also known as de Bouchard) does well on the east-facing side of the garden. On the shaded west-facing wall another pink, 'Hagley Hybrid', flourishes, together with deep violet 'Jackmanii', 'F.H. Young', which is a little paler, and perhaps best of all, the soft lavender 'Mrs Cholmondeley'. If you like 'Nelly Moser', she keeps her stripes better out of the sun. For a large area of shaded wall, the twining montanas are excellent, with attractive foliage and drifts of white or pink flowers in spring: some, such as 'Elizabeth', 'Tetrarose' and 'Wilsonii' are fragrant. They grow vigorously, reaching twenty or thirty feet (6–9m) and look their best when given plenty of space – wonderful when allowed to ramble through a tree.

TOP LEFT: Philadelphus coronaria *'Aureus' prefers light shade where its leaves retain their lovely colour and the white flowers scent the air.*

TOP RIGHT: *In mild and sheltered areas, the evergreen climber,* Clematis armandii, *produces its deliciously scented white flowers profusely, even in shade.*

The early-flowering *Clematis macropetala*, a delicate-looking thing, is as tough as can be; I am particularly fond of the fern-like leaves and small, nodding flowers of violet, pink or white, which are followed by silky seed-heads. *Clematis alpina* is rather similar, flowering in April and May. Both of these, together with the montanas, are described as fully hardy, and suitable for exposed and shaded sites. In sun or shade, all clematis need moisture; prepare the planting holes thoroughly, with good compost and a little bonemeal.

The climbing hydrangea, *Hydrangea anomala* ssp. *petiolaris*, is a rugged, self-clinging plant. In the winter its sturdy trunk and branches fan out over the walls so that it seems the house is lovingly cradled by a hirsute giant; in summer the heart-shaped leaves and lace-mat corymbs are charming. Winter jasmine (*Jasminum nudiflorum*) should be given some support; plant it where it can be seen from the house so that its small yellow flowers, scattered like stars against the green leaves, lift our hearts on the dreariest days. No scent, alas, whereas the deciduous *Jasminum officinale* is very fragrant and quite happy here.

Although I am not mad about ungainly bushes of deciduous forsythia in a small garden, *Forsythia suspensa* is a graceful thing, up to about fifteen feet (4.5m) if trained on a wall; particularly good is *F.s. atrocaulis*, with pale, lemon-yellow flowers on purplish-black branches in spring.

The woodbine, *Lonicera periclymenum*, has all the fragrance associated with the family; like most honeysuckles, it is happy in shade and will twine itself round anything in reach. Late and early Dutch honeysuckles extend the season and two other good but unscented ones are *Lonicera tragophylla* with pale yellow flowers and *Lonicera* x *tellmanniana* with yellowy-orange flowers. Creamy-flowered *Lonicera japonica* 'Halliana' is evergreen and scented but has to be watched to ensure that it does not strangle everything in sight; if not cut back regularly it becomes a dense mass of twigs under a thin canopy of leaves and flowers.

I try to like that most most popular of plants, the pyracantha: it is an obliging evergreen in sun and shade, with white flowers and bead-like berries of bright red, orange or yellow which are beloved by the birds; it may be a free-standing shrub or trained over walls and ugly sheds – what more could one ask? I have struggled too often among its vicious branches to forgive, but as it seems to be increasingly susceptible to blight, my revenge may be near.

On the other hand, ivies I love dearly, for they are amenable plants that perform in the most awkward corners, nor do they bite the hands that feed and prune. *Hedera helix* seems unfairly named as the common ivy, for it has a distinguished appearance, grown as ground cover, up an old tree or over the house walls. In the adult stage, the greenish flowers appear, a great attraction to moths, bees and butterflies. 'Goldheart' (now known as *Heder*a 'Oro di Bogliasco', alas) is particularly useful as it keeps its variegation in the shade and will make a golden splash up a dark wall.

For autumn colour, the deciduous, tendril-climbing *Parthenocissus henryana* is an elegant creature, reaching right up to the gutters, and draping swags of silvery-veined green leaves as it goes, colouring up to a glowing red when autumn comes. I get the benefit of my neighbour's plant dangling over my bathroom window; it takes a good deal of light, throwing the room into a green shade, but how pleasant to take one's bath like Sabrina 'under the glassy-green, translucent wave' in summer, and later in the year watch its brilliant transformation into its autumn red.

This is by no means a complete list of climbers (vines) for a shaded garden. Everyone has their own favourites and while some stalwarts will appear on most lists, others will be on only one or two. So much depends on soil type, climate, light, shelter, the heat from the house, etc.; most important of all, the preparation of the soil and the aftercare.

When the wall covering plants are in place, add the rest of the shrubs. Those with glossy leaves are particular valuable in shade, for they too reflect light. If you have the space for it, *Fatsia japonica* is like an evergreen fig-tree, the shiny, deeply lobed leaves casting fantastic shadows. It grows to twelve to thirteen feet (4m) and, in late autumn, has rounded white flower heads, followed by small black fruit; the variegated form is very showy, its leaves creamily margined. Both are excellent in town gardens.

Equally bold, the winter-flowering evergreen *Mahonia japonica* is tough and fragrant. *Mahonia* 'Charity' has long, spiny leaves: in winter, its long, yellow racemes smell strongly of lilies-of-the-valley. In time it can grow to ten feet (3m) high and wide, but may be cut back; one flower head, surrounded by its ruff of leaves, makes a remarkable centrepiece for the dining-table, scenting the room gloriously.

Few plants are as forgiving as the aucubas; long out of fashion and derided as mere 'spotted laurels', they are now deservedly back in favour. Evergreen, growing to about ten feet (3m) in time, tolerant of shade, drought, poor soil and pollution, their polished, gold-freckled leaves and sealing-wax berries (does anyone now use sealing-wax?) make them very desirable in sophisticated planting schemes and containers.

Lower-growing, up to a yard or a little more, skimmias are excellent shade-plants; evergreen with fragrant white flowers in early spring, followed by bright scarlet berries. You need both male and female plants to get a good crop of berries, *Skimmia* 'Rubella' being a useful male with a reddish tinge to its flower heads. Like the aucubas, when small they make excellent plants for shaded winter windowboxes and containers.

Evergreen *Viburnum tinus* flowers all winter, its small, dark green leaves a perfect foil for the white flower heads, which are even better when cut and brought into the house; on their own, in a jug or bowl, they are invaluable when so few other flowers are about: 'Eve Price' and 'Gwenllian' are good forms and I am fond of *V.t.* 'Variegatum', with creamy-yellow-edged leaves, which looks especially well in shade. *Viburnum davidii*, which produces blue berries, is another excellent plant. The Mexican orange, *Choisya ternata*, flourishes almost as well here, in mild, temperate climates, as it does in sun, even when grown under trees. If crowded, its growth becomes weak and straggly, but apart from that it is very accommodating, having glossy, aromatic evergreen leaves and masses of scented white flowers in spring, followed by others throughout the year. It makes a large bush, but can be cut back regularly.

Camellias, especially the frost-hardy *Camellia japonica* and its cultivars, are some of the finest plants for a lightly shaded town garden, except in the coldest zones. The gleaming foliage is distinguished all year and the flowers, when they come, are of great beauty. Growing happily in a container for some years, reaching six feet (1.8m) or so, in the ground they can make great bushes or small trees; they like a neutral to acid soil, with plenty of leafmould and peat or peat substitutes.

Ornamental quinces (*Chaenomeles*) are a delight in the spring, grown as a free-standing shrub or trained along a wall, with red, white, pink or coral flowers, followed by yellow fruit. I love the white 'Nivalis' best of all. In the park here there are many quinces huddled among other shrubs in the quite dense shade of old plane trees: it is a delight to spot the first buds, like little jewels on the bare branches, and watch them open up into small, glowing cups. When the flowers are gone and the leaves are out, the shrubs fade back into the general greenery, only to reappear in autumn when the golden quinces hang like small, fat lanterns on the black twigs.

Morello cherries grow well on a shaded wall, but it is a struggle to keep birds away from the blossom. It is an odd thing – in one garden birds will ravish everything in sight while in another near by, they flit about happily without attacking the flowers at all. In mine, for instance, the sparrows leave the polyanthus alone for a while, but then I wake up to find these chomped down to the leaves; next the leaves go too. Meanwhile, a friend who lives in the next street has no such problems – her polyanthus bloom away so merrily that I could spit.

I would not be without some clumps of bamboo, the less invasive kinds, in this shaded part of the garden. They look well in a clump on their own, their leaves casting shadows on the walls and paving, but also adding interest to mixed planting schemes, and particularly good near water.

Tucked in between the climbers (vines) and shrubs are the smaller things that will take some shade: alchemillas with foam-flowers of acid yellow; early-flowering bergenias with round, evergreen leaves; the prostrate campanulas with their blue bell-flowers; cranesbills; silver-streaked dead-nettles;

BOTTOM LEFT:
Mahonia *'Charity' is a useful shrub that does well in shade. Of architectural character, with handsome evergreen leaves, in winter and spring it bears long yellow racemes with a strong lily-of-the-valley fragrance.*

BOTTOM RIGHT:
Viburnum tinus *tolerates shade, pollution and neglect although it will repay any kindness it is shown. V.* tinus *'Gwenllian' is pictured here.*

epimediums with their small, heart-shaped leaves; euphorbias, ferns, foxgloves, delicate fuchsias; hellebores with handsome leaves and freckle-faced flowers of white, green and palest pink to darkest purple; honesty; all the lovely hostas (if you can keep the slugs at bay) with their handsome leaves which may be green, gold, glaucous-blue or strikingly variegated; the tall, late-flowering Japanese anemones; lilies-of-the-valley, London pride, periwinkles, Solomon's seal – the list goes on and is full of modest beauties.

As to bulbs and so on, I like to see them tucked into any bare earth: small daffodils, delicate-looking *Anemone nemorosa*, the autumn-flowering *Cyclamen hederifolium*, spring-flowering *Cyclamen coum*, and little, yellow-flowered, green-frilled winter aconites growing under the bare branches of deciduous shrubs and trees. I plant clumps of *Anemone blanda*, snowdrops, snowflakes, grape hyacinths and bluebells (though these last can be something of a weed in a small garden) wherever I can. And lilies – one could not be without them; many, martagon lilies and regales in particular, will take some shade, while most like to have their roots in it, growing up to the light through lower plants. I find containers the best way to grow them in town gardens; they can be moved about, breathtaking when in flower, and tucked away in a quiet corner when not.

Annuals are the last to go in and they bring green, shaded gardens into sharp focus: busy-lizzies, fibrous-rooted begonias, fuchsias and tobacco plants do especially well, but many others will perform more than adequately as long as they get at least some light. Every year I am torn: whether to fill the pots with cool green and white or to overflow them with wicked colour. Green shade, delicious as it is, need not be all.

Above the walls the west light hangs, until
The White Tea roses, staying where deep shade is,
Ghosts of old lovely ladies,
Whisper and stir till all the flowers fill
The living darkness with a sense of sound.

DOROTHY, DUCHESS OF WELLINGTON (1889–1936)

7

ALL GLORIOUS WITHIN

Courtyards

Save it was closed well, I you ensure,
With masonry of compass environ
Full secretly, with satires going down.
In midst the place, a turning wheel, certayne,
And upon that, a pot of margoleyne.

ANON. (FIFTEENTH CENTURY)

OPPOSITE: *Trailing foliage, white lilies and hydrangeas surround the pool and wall fountain in this attractive blue and white courtyard. Mrs Robert Chandler's garden.* (DESIGNERS Matthew West, Nigel Manton and Elizabeth Chandler)

COURTYARD — it has a romantic sound and, indeed, has romantic roots; the early meaning was that of an open area, surrounded by walls or buildings, set within the precincts of a castle, great house or religious foundation. It was in such enclosed areas, safe from the dangerous world outside, that gardening as we know it began. Now the word is more likely to refer to something that in many cases might just as well be called a backyard (rather a pejorative word in Britain, though in America it refers to perfectly respectable, often sizable gardens). Courtyard, atrium, backyard, patio or side-passage (sideyard): no matter how small, these are still safe and sheltered places.

Today's courtyard is usually a small area at the back, and just occasionally at the front or side, of a town house; with luck the surrounding walls may be no more than about six to eight feet (2m) high, but sometimes one or all of them may be considerably taller, which does pose special problems. Similar gardens are also, though less often, found in villages and, increasingly, in new housing developments (condominiums).

Another, comparatively recent practice is the splitting up of large houses into smaller units and the conversion of outbuildings, such as garages, stables, barns and so on, into separate habitations, many of which have a walled or stable-yard garden. For the purposes of this chapter, *courtyard* is taken to include all of these; also basement areas and those small, internal light-wells at the base of tall buildings, the only space available to some and all the more precious for that.

Wherever they are and whatever the size, there is a great deal that may be done with them and the transformation can be a gratifying process: the more unpromising things are at the start, the greater the satisfaction at the finish. As always, one begins by assessing the pluses and minuses of the area. A dank, airless feeling is most likely when the area is particularly small, shaded and surrounded by very high walls that tend to hinder the free circulation of the air. Regular clean-ups are specially

A low-maintenance courtyard or lightwell.

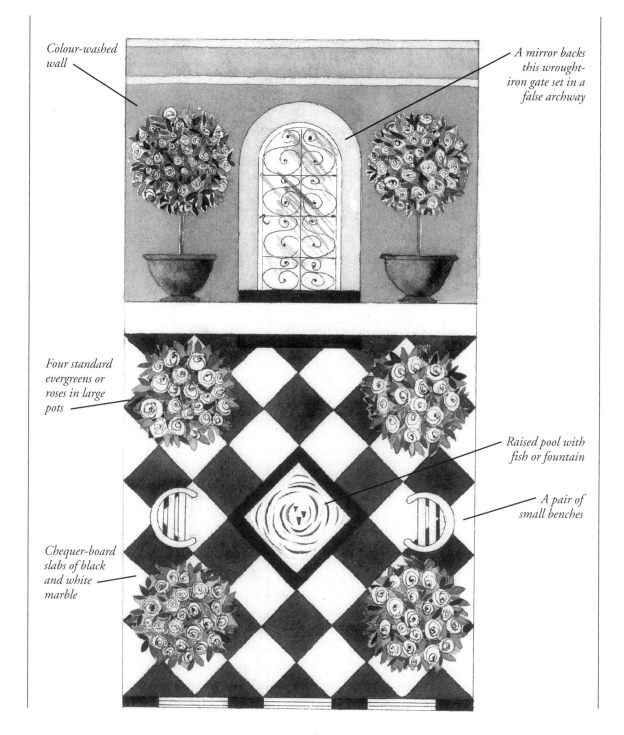

Colour-washed wall

A mirror backs this wrought-iron gate set in a false archway

Four standard evergreens or roses in large pots

Raised pool with fish or fountain

A pair of small benches

Chequer-board slabs of black and white marble

necessary here to remove all debris that might harbour plant-pests and diseases. There is unlikely to be much of a view, except perhaps in the country, where the odd glimpse of treetops or a distant church may be caught; the 'view' must therefore be created within.

The walls are nearly always an asset, or have the makings of one. Courtyards are likely to be sheltered from harsh winds: even in the shade they will benefit from the warmth of the surrounding houses, enabling many tender plants to be grown. Sun is a plus, but shade need not be a minus; simply more of a challenge. Occasionally there will be some in-built advantage: a beautiful small tree, a handsome doorway or window, architectural details such as decorative brickwork, an inviting archway or a waiting alcove. More often, we are presented with a blank canvas, just a few yards of concrete and the bare walls.

Once again, we must consider whether the garden is primarily a view from a window, a place for private relaxation, or somewhere to entertain: an outdoor dining-room, or a convenient venue for a drinks party. If the latter (which may be determined by size), an uncluttered centre is desirable.

'The very small dark plot perhaps only a few square feet, in the heart of the city appears, at a gardener's first glance, an almost hopeless situation; that is, if he has hopes of gardening it in the conventional sense of the word. But such sites are really quite easy to transform if one looks at them from a different point of view. One has to garden them by allusion, first of all creating a sense of space and volume and then emphasizing the mood towards which you are aiming,' wrote Russell Page; once again, we must consult the *genius loci*, assess the ambience. An urban, rural or coastal site will, to some extent, determine that, as will the surroundings and the architecture of the house. Because of the tight geometry, the design is likely to lean towards the formal or even the minimalist, but not necessarily so. The styles of many ages and many countries are available to us. Grecian and Roman classicism, ornate Moorish-Spanish cool, Scandinavian simplicity or laid-back Californian; monastic or erotic, romantic or high-tech ... and so on; worldwide, there is a courtyard for all tastes.

If the walls are of stone or mellowed brick and in good condition, leave them as they are, a dignified background for the climbing plants, but repair any defective patches first. Stucco, concrete and undistinguished brickwork need a coat or two of paint. Ideally, give concrete blocks and any really poor walls a finish of cement-render (stucco) before applying paint. An absolutely smooth finish is not necessary: imperfections add character, but do not let the plasterers finish it all off with rustic swirls as they will long to do.

Trellis is used to screen poor walls; but even on perfect walls it is decorative and a useful plant-support. Fit it all round the courtyard walls or add individual panels where needed; use 'illusion' trellis panels for the impression of a recessed arch or to frame a mirror, statue or vase (planted or unplanted) on a pedestal.

Ugly pipe runs are a problem, particularly in basement areas. Hide them with trellis or paint the pipes to match or blend with the walls and obliterate them with climbers (vines).

Old planks or rolls of split bamboo canes are good disguises for indifferent walls: the first gives an informal, rustic feel and the latter, a discreet nod in the direction of the Orient.

As elsewhere, choose colours for the paintwork to affect the mood of the courtyard. Perhaps

OPPOSITE: *The deep blue of the back wall shows off the trailing wall-plants, the bronze spikes of the cordyline and the leaves and leaning trunk of a young fig tree. Extra colour is provided by the plants grown in containers clustered on the unusual cobbled steps.* (DESIGNER Ann Frith)

white walls are the first thought; they have a bright, crisp charm, making a good background for almost all foliage and for flowers of whatever hue. Pastel shades, of pink, blue, cream, fawn, yellow and green for instance, are soft and fresh, bestowing an impression of light, even if there is not much about. Black and the darker blues, greens, browns and reds give a more aware, sophisticated look, while rosy and tawny tints or sunny yellows make for warmth. Evergreens and other dark plants show to advantage in front of a pale or warm wall; against a dark background those with pale, silver, gold or variegated foliage will be most striking.

Climbing roses, wisteria, clematis, grape-vines, honeysuckle and many other wall-plants (vines) of medium vigour can be trained round the walls and over the trellis, but if the air circulation is poor it will be even more necessary than usual to spray against disease. In a small yard, train one or two plants into a living trellis or let them encircle a round window or a wall plaque to give these more importance.

The mood of the courtyard will be affected by the architectural details, the choice of plants and the colours on doors, windows, shutters, furniture, containers and all other odds and ends, functional or ornamental. Coloured fabrics play their part – sun-blinds, parasols, tablecloths and cushions, etc. All these will add up to a satisfactory whole if well handled.

Take, for example, a shady, sunken courtyard where no attempt is made to disguise the resulting gloom; rather, it is emphasized. The walls are painted a distinguished shade of slate-blue, at the far end is an immense arched mirror, over which hangs a pair of fearsome horns; in front of the glass is a piece of contemporary sculpture. Ivy, camellias, skimmias and other glossy-leaved evergreen shrubs, underplanted with masses of white busy-lizzies, the only light touch allowed, fill the raised beds that line the two side walls. The table and chairs are painted black, yet the effect is not at all funereal but arresting. At night, when pierced-brass lanterns throw intricate patterns of light and shade, it is deliciously surreal.

Or imagine a sunny courtyard with walls of rosy terracotta. Against one wall place a blue-grey bench and fix the windows with shutters painted the same shade. Flank the bench with a pair of box (boxwood) spirals planted either directly into the ground or in terracotta pots. The garden will look interesting throughout the year but need little maintenance. Adding pots of spring bulbs, lilies and seasonal annuals will give scent and extra colour, while a climber (vine) or two might be trained over the walls. Grape-vines or passion-flowers would be charming, given something to cling to. Self-clinging ivy and the twining evergreen, Chilean bellflower (*Lapageria rosea*), with its fleshy red or pink flowers, will thrive on the shaded sides, together with some of the others described in the last chapter. If we paint everything ourselves, use old bricks and gravel for the ground surface and grow plants from seeds and cuttings, it will be quite an economical garden to establish, even taking into account the cost of the topiary and the bench.

Think of other colour combinations and different topiary shapes. Pale yellow walls, a white bench and a pair of mop-headed *Cupressus arizonica glabra* , with foliage like verdigris, would be soft and pretty. For an urbane sparkle, try white walls, a dark green bench; in summer, replace the topiary with standard marguerites (*Argyranthemum frutescens*) in Versailles *caisses,* underplanted by

scarlet geraniums. Replace the Versailles *caisses* with dark green tubs and the red geraniums with pink ones, for a softer, more rustic feel.

On the sunny side one might add one or two evergreen climbers (vines) such as the white-flowered *Pileostegia viburnoides*, and *Sollya heterophylla*, which has narrow, shiny leaves and small, nodding, bluebell flowers from early spring to late autumn, or rather it does in my garden here,

SCENTED PLANTS

TREES AND TREE-LIKE SHRUBS		PERENNIALS	TENDER PERENNIALS, ANNUALS AND BIENNIALS
Azara Z8	Daphne (several)	Wisteria, to Z4	Erysimum
Clerodendrun, to Z7	Elaeagnus (some)		Heliotropium
Cytisus battandieri Z8	Mahonia (most)	**PERENNIALS**	Lobularia maritima
Drimys winteri Z8	Osmanthus, to Z6	Aurinia Z3	Matthiola incana
Ligustrum, to Z7	Pittosporum tobira Z9	Convallaria Z3	Nicotiana
Magnolia (several, both deciduous and evergreen)	Rhododendron luteum	Cosmos atrosanguineus Z8	Petunia (some)
	Sarcococca Z6	Dianthus (many)	Verbena (some)
Malus (some)	Skimmia Z7	Hemerocallis (some, esp. yellow cvs.), to Z4	Viola (some)
Philadelphus (most)	Viburnum (several)		
Prunus (some)		Iris graminea	**BULBS**
Syringa (many)	**CLIMBERS**	I. unguicularis	Hyacinthoides non-scripta
	Clematis armandii	Lupinus (many)	Hyacinthus orientalis
SHRUBS	C. flammula Z6	Monarda didyma	Lilium (most)
Abelia Z5	C. montana (most) Z6	Primula (some)	Narcissus (many)
Buddleja (several), to Z5	Jasminum (most)	Viola odorata Z8	Scilla
Choisya Z7	Lonicera (most)		
	Trachelospermum jasminoides Z9		

where it has come through some quite sharp frosts. Most of the plants mentioned in the chapter on a sunny garden would thrive on the walls of such a courtyard. Because the conditions are so sheltered, it is worth trying all kinds of exotic things, for sun or shade, that might not otherwise be hardy in the locality.

There are other interesting ways in which to enliven the walls: with plaques, collages, wall-tiles, masks, mirrors, murals and *trompe l'oeil*. Consider a wildly exotic mural of tropical plants, a convincing *trompe l'oeil* featuring a landscape or architectural feature (a flight of steps, a pillared portico, a painted window, complete with curtains and a cat, dog or other interested observer peering out), a tree full of doves, and so on.

One wall entirely covered by mirror and edged with plants gives a spacious feel; a series of mirrored arches round all the walls conveys something of the cloister. If the mirrors are salvaged, the expense is not so great. Or transform a dull yard by adding stencilled garlands of bay leaves, swags of ivy or trailing vines. In one basement area, we painted arches round the walls and gave each alternate arch painted cut-outs of orange and lemon trees in pots. Try a tawny-yellow wall, grey-green pots or tubs, and at Christmas, add gilded fruit and nuts. These painted schemes are excellent where there is little light, space or time for maintenance: they are particularly useful in narrow passage or side gardens (sideyards), taking up little space. In such areas, walls are almost all there is to work with, so use them to the full. Every detail counts. Here the flatter ornaments come into their own – picturesque shutters, mirrors, plaques, tile 'pictures', murals of all kinds, small, self-contained wall-fountains and so on.

If possible, make narrow beds along the base of the walls or build some raised planters there; failing this, slim containers will be the answer. Lighting makes a vast difference; space-saving wall-lanterns are decorative as well as useful. A wider side garden can be treated much like the regular courtyards just described.

'The floor beneath was paved fair and smooth, with stones square of many divers hues ...'

There is the courtyard floor to consider. Quality of soil is not so significant here, as in most cases the planting areas will be non-existent or very small. If the floor surface is poor, it may be best to break it up and start again, but when this is not feasible, an inch or so of gravel or shingle will cover a multitude of faults. When the courtyard floor is satisfactory it is sensible and economical to leave it undisturbed, and plant in raised beds or containers, filled with good topsoil or commercial composts (soil mixes).

While grass is technically possible, it seldom looks convincing and is generally impractical. The combination of shade and congested foot-traffic in a small area will prevent it from thriving, while there is unlikely to be space for a mower. If you must have grass, let it be in a pattern of small raised beds where it can be replaced annually, and be clipped and watered by hand; this looks fresh and pretty.

The courtyard floor is often the main feature of the design. Paving slabs or tiles are ideal in a town setting. Cool marble squares and brightly coloured tiles from Spain, Portugal and Mexico are at home in a small sunny courtyard, perhaps one with a shallow central pool and a fountain; the sound of water is an essential ingredient of the perfect courtyard.

The effect of square paving-units may be varied by setting them in straight or diamond-shaped courses, but we are seldom after movement, illusion or 'stretching' devices here. Rather, the pattern is used to concentrate our attention within, playing much the same visual role as a good rug in a small room, often having a border and a central motif (a circle, diamond, star, fish, entwined initials, etc.). A chequerboard floor within, say, a Greek-key border always looks handsome but other ideas can be gained by studying carpets, tiles, mosaics and so on. Mosaic is effective but needs a good eye and an expert hand to do well.

Stone, slate, terracotta and quarry tiles (all tiles should be frost-proof where necessary), stable pavers, granite setts, bricks, gravel and timber decking all look well in the right place. Small flattish pebbles and stones make an excellent surface, either over the whole area or inset as patterns among other materials. On a smooth cement floor, paintwork checks or patterns are economical and striking. There are special paints for this work and stencils make it easier to execute the more elaborate designs.

In a rural courtyard, all these materials would be suitable, with the exception, perhaps, of marble and the more colourful ceramics, while decking, old planks, railway sleepers (cross-ties), cobbles and crushed shells are at home there. In the country, too, one can get away with crazy paving (random flagstones) but even here it looks best when combined with other materials, as for example, laid within a brick or timber-edged square, diamond or circle.

Where space allows add small formal beds of roses, annuals, herbs, saladings, etc., making a geometric pattern or knot-garden of some kind, with or without some ornamental thing at the centre: a seat (or a pair of them), sculpture, vase, well-head, raised bed, pool or fountain perhaps.

All the formal shapes can be used for both pools and raised beds, but round, hexagonal or octagonal ones are particularly suitable, taking up less space than others for a comparable surface area; given a wide coping, these double as space-saving seats. A pool against a wall takes up even less room. A triangular pool set across a corner (or one in all four corners, for that matter) is interesting. Backed by mirrors, the various wall-pools appear to be full-sized circles, squares or rectangles, with further gardens beyond.

Small canals are charming here, whether single, double or cross-shaped, echoing the Islamic design. Wall-fountains are ideal in a really tiny yard or light well and a small bubbling fountain, falling over pebbles into a concealed reservoir below, would be pleasant, although I shall not mourn if I never again see another of those ubiquitous millstone fountains, or another burping oil jar. Better to edge the sunken tank with a neat circle of bricks, tiles, granite setts or clipped evergreens, then spread cobbles, small stones, slate pebbles, shells or even glass marbles over the grid-cover, adjusting the jet so that the water bubbles up through and over them in a neatly restrained fashion.

Where there is room for it, a small tree or tree-like shrub makes a good centrepiece for a largish courtyard. Let it be one with special qualities and year-long appeal. All shapely or 'architectural' varieties are worth considering. Keep within the allotted space by rubbing out a bud here, pinching a young shoot there and giving a discreet annual trim. Light them at night for extra magic. Evergreen plants are always a good choice, for their winter interest and the gleam of their leaves. Where the climate allows, citrus trees have all the virtues, being evergreen, glossy and fragrant, while bearing flowers and edible fruit; an arbutus has similar but more rugged charms.

Consider, too, those plants with polished bark, coloured stems or twisted trunks and branches; also those with a weeping habit, bright foliage, berries and, whenever possible, scented flowers. Trees and shrubs with handsome leaves that throw constantly shifting shadows on walls and floor prove a perennial source of dramatic interest; figs, fatsias and aralias come to mind.

The weeping Kilmarnock willow fits into a tiny yard; so too the evergreen, red-berried *Cotoneaster* x *suecicus* 'Coral Beauty', trained as a weeping standard; topiary work would be perfect. Most of the smaller standard roses mentioned in the planting chapter could be charming. A small weeping crab-apple or cherry tree are suitable, given a fraction more space. In half-shade, try a delicate, cut-leafed Japanese maple, or, in a slightly larger courtyard, the starry-flowered, deciduous magnolia, *M. stellata*, or a glossy camellia. The evergreen *Cotoneaster salicifolius* 'Pendulus' or the purple willow, *Salix purpurea* 'Pendula', are both delightful here.

Raised beds are invaluable; somewhere between twelve and eighteen inches (30–45cm) is about right in most cases, but the height may vary within the site. Bricks, blocks, planks, old timbers (lumber) or railway sleepers (cross-ties) can be used but anything self-consciously 'rustic', such as rolls of cut logs or shaggy stonework, would be out of place. Local stone looks right in villages and country towns or by the sea. If the walls are wide enough or have a broad coping they make a useful seat. Take care when building raised beds against the house: either leave a gap of a few inches, or install efficient damp-proofing.

Children present special problems in such a small space. It might be best to turn the whole area over to them during the day and reclaim it for the adults at night when, in theory at least, the children will be abed (do today's children *ever* go to bed?). No matter how limited the space, it should be possible to have climbing-ropes and a swing (which can, if necessary, be unhooked at

---

AROMATIC PLANTS

TREES	Artemisia	Phlomis	Artemisia
Eucalyptus	Choisya	Rosmarinus	Mentha
Laurus nobilis	Cistus	Salvia officinalis	Monarda didyma
and many conifers	Helichrysum italicum	Thymus	Nepeta
	Lavandula		Origanum
SHRUBS	Myrtus	**PERENNIALS**	Pelargonium (scented-leaved)
Aloysia citriodora	Perovskia	Acorus calamus	Tanacetum parthenium

---

night) slung from an overhead beam spanning the side walls or a corner of them. A small covered sandpit, with a removable cushion on top, doubles as a low seat. Any sunny corner makes a good place for a paddling pool, one that can be emptied and stowed away at the drop of a hat. Failing a paddling pool, place a shallow tray for water-play on a low table which can be appropriated later for wine, glasses and so on. Older children will enjoy a netball or basketball ring, hung high. Artificial grass is fine as a ground surface here, comfortable for the children and quite acceptable in this kind of artificial situation. Alternatively, given a smooth concrete floor, one might paint the floor and make the entire yard a chess-board, a track for model cars or a giant hopscotch grid. Children love to have their own gardens so here start them off with a pot or an old sink, some good soil and some unobtrusive help.

There should be an outside water-supply. Containers need frequent soaking, while plants grown in raised beds require more water, more often, than those in the open ground, so an automatic watering-system would be helpful. In towns especially, dusty or grimy walls, floors, furniture, plants and children require hosing-down from time to time. This in turn necessitates an adequate drainage system; there will probably be one there already, but check that it functions properly and is not obstructed in any way.

The courtyard takes on a new lease of life at night; run extra lights and a fountain-pump off a low-voltage cable. When the existing floor stays, run cables round the base of the walls; if starting from scratch, thread them through conduits beneath whatever paving is being installed. In addition to the regular lighting effects, unusual wall-lights or lanterns are attractive and throw interesting patterns of light and shade; a dimmer switch is useful. Hide wiring behind trellis and trailing plants or chase into the walls. Those strings of tiny white lights are very pretty here, hung overhead or threaded along the branches of small trees.

Storage-space for toys, cushions, tools, hose, fertilizers, etc., is always a problem in a courtyard, except in those rare instances where an existing small building is decorative enough to be retained. Some old houses still have an outside privy: these make excellent tool-sheds, so one should cherish them. Usually built in the same weathered brickwork as that of the house, under a slate or tiled roof, with a painted door of tongue-and-groove boards, they fade pleasantly and obtrusively into the background but may be embellished by climbing plants (vines). In courtyards reached by stairs from above, a discreet cupboard goes neatly beneath the steps.

Where there is room, make a small pavilion or false portico against the far wall as a sheltered and decorative place to sit, with storage-space hidden at the sides or under the seats. Simplest of all, erect a fine-meshed trellis panel as a screen across one corner so that tools can be kept there in a plastic container or sacks to keep them dry.

A wooden storage-bench is useful: a long box with a hinged lid, about eighteen inches (45cm) high and wide, by something between three and six feet (90 x 180cm) long. Paint or stain it and keep its cushions inside the bench when not in use.

When raised beds run round the walls, incorporate a seating-area with one or two loose slabs supported on the brickwork so that odds and ends can be tucked away in the cavity beneath. This is a great space-saver, looks neat when integrated into the overall design and is surprisingly comfortable when fat cushions are added.

In the very tiniest yards, a large pot or half-barrel makes a miniature storage-space for a garden hose, a trowel, hand-fork, secateurs, gardening gloves, a packet of slug pellets and the odd bottle of liquid manure. Cut a circle out of plywood (exterior quality) to fit over the top and paint to match; over that goes either a cushion or a lightweight, shallow container, planted up with rock-plants, ivy or low-growing annuals.

When the garden is hot or is overlooked, you can make a small creeper-covered pergola to give some shade and privacy, but whenever possible, a courtyard should be left open to the sky. A small pavilion or an open-fronted and pillared garden-house at one end would be a better plan; raise it on a brick semicircle, for such a change of level, however slight, works well even in these small spaces (it may also be used as a base for a seat or an ornament of some kind, either centrally or against a wall).

Basement areas and light-wells have a particular need for cheer, as often they receive little sun; once again bright paintwork and any of the various treatments previously described should do the trick. In very deep light-wells, use overhead trellis to bring down the 'sky' to a comfortable level and screen out the high walls and drain-pipes without taking too much of the light.

In one small well we covered the walls with mirror-glass to a height of eight feet (240cm) and this in turn was covered with trellis. A white Versailles box was placed in each of the four corners, planted with a camellia of upright habit, more for the glossy leaves than for any possible flowers. Matching troughs filled with skimmias ran round the walls. In summer, we added a folding café table and two chairs. White busy-lizzies were used to fill gaps in the troughs and a couple of pots of standard white daisies were set on either side of the French windows. The feeling of claustrophobic gloom was successfully overcome; from a wasted space it became a valued and much-used little garden.

Another difficult area was a small, deep basement yard, narrow and L-shaped. The first leg ran past the kitchen window. This kitchen was also used as an informal dining- and sitting-room, so the outlook was important. We placed a large trough, with two climbers (vines), evergreen shrubs and white annuals on the opposite wall where it could be seen from within, then set a few pots on either side of the window, so that the flowers and foliage framed it. Just to one side, but still in view, we added a marble boy who balanced a flower pot on his shoulder and this we filled with campanulas.

OPPOSITE RIGHT: *An eye-catching treatment for a dull wall, with white paint, decorative trellis, three round finials, a mop-headed standard of clipped box in a swagged terracotta pot and a large-leaved, variegated ivy.* (DESIGNER Anthony Noel)

OPPOSITE LEFT: *Roses, fuchsias, hydrangeas, a small bench and a miniature jungle of trailing foliage completely transform this narrow alley alongside a town house. (The Hon. Julia Stonor's garden)*

Other troughs, similarly planted, continued round the walls. Two or three chimney pots, filled with drooping fuchsias and trailing ivies, added height. A brick arch was made across the wall at the far end of the other, more shaded leg, forming an alcove. This we painted a deep, tawny red as a back-drop for a noble Roman, in theory far too large for such a tiny garden, but actually the very making of it.

In one last example, a large but rather gloomy basement apartment was for sale but attracted no buyers. It had three small open areas; in desperation, the owners painted all the walls white and bought some pleasant but inexpensive containers. In the front, by the steps, they built a large raised bed of old bricks. This they planted with a yellow catalpa and a large wisteria, which clambered up the railings, then crammed any remaining spaces with green-and-gold trailing ivies and white annu-als. The middle, narrowest area had just two small cement vases, painted white, each planted with a tall pyramid of silver-green ivy. Between them stood a marble statute, a junk-shop find. The third,

A small, trellised pavilion, draped with roses, gives shade and shelter in a sunny corner. (DESIGNER Christopher Masson)

slightly larger area outside the kitchen had a marble table and slender metal chairs, also junk-shop buys. Here were the largest containers, filled with bamboos, fatsias, camellias, nandina, feathery Japanese maples and a mass of pastel annuals. The plants and containers cost quite a bit but within a week the place was sold; sometimes a little extravagance pays off.

In such shaded spots, architectural plants and those with glossy or variegated leaves are very effective. I have found the following particularly useful: aucuba, bamboo, bergenia, camellia, variegated dogwood *(Cornus alba* 'Elegantissima'), euonymus, fatsias (the variegated form is attractive), ferns, fuchsia, hellebore, hosta, hydrangea, ivies (both plain green and variegated), Japanese maples, privet, small rhododendrons and evergreen azaleas, skimmia, *Viburnum davidii* and *V. tinus.*

Most courtyards, in sun or shade, benefit from a few pots of lilies and other bulbs, seasonal annuals and other small things to provide scent and colour. All the plants needed can be grown in containers, allowing those with different requirements to flourish. The containers and the plants in them should be chosen with the same care as all the other elements of the courtyard to be in sympathy with its overall mood. At such close quarters, they will be the making or the marring of it. If in doubt, keep everything simple.

Once again Russell Page puts it well. 'On a very small site, one perhaps where the whole garden area is no bigger than that of the house, I would always tend to treat it as one more large room, that has the sky for its ceiling ... each shrub or small tree would be carefully chosen for its shape and texture, and the flowers I chose to use would conform to a scheme of colour of which one would not tire too quickly. Sometimes one is lucky enough to hit on a formula, a combination of colour, texture and shape, which looks so inevitable and right that it becomes "classical". It is this quality of fitness for its place that I would always look for in working out the planting for such an outdoor room.'

Goodly it was enclosed round about,
As well their entred guestes to keepe within,
As those unruly beasts to hold without.

ANON. (FIFTEENTH CENTURY)

8

WIND, STARS AND HIGH HOPES

Roof Gardens

> *petunias*
> > *tubs of pink petunias*
> *a grey roof*
> > *black when it's hot*
> *light greys today*
> > *green tubs of punctured glow*
> > > *before a glowing wall*
> *all the walls reflecting light*
> *at six on a summer evening*

JAMES SCHUYLER (1933–)

*O*F ALL THE UNLIKELY PLACES in which town-dwellers struggle to make a garden, wrestling a green and atavistically reassuring retreat out of the barren surroundings, surely a roof is the most ridiculous, the most surreal. But that gives us the clue, for whatever style we aim for, whatever pretty illusions are contrived, there is the underlying awareness that we perch in a bizarre eyrie, vulnerable to the elements, bereft of neighbours and unnervingly close to heaven. Gardening on high is unashamedly artificial; we should enjoy it on those terms, as a deliciously unnatural vice, a special and secret delight to be indulged in until the roof becomes at last one of those true 'gloriettas of the individual man', in Sylvia Crowe's charming phrase.

But here the practicalities must come first. Is the roof strong enough for our plans? Will it support a couple of tubs, let alone anything of a Babylonian nature? If there is any doubt about this, call in experts before going further; no matter how light the containers and the dry compost (soil mix) may be, once the latter is soaked the weight will be considerable.

A strong concrete roof makes virtually everything possible – stone or marble statues, pools, paving-slabs, pergolas, etc.; while raised beds or large planters can go anywhere, not just round the edges where the roof is strongest.

Asphalt softens in hot weather, causing furniture and containers to sink through and allowing water to leak into the rooms below. Screed over or cover with lightweight tiles. Decking spreads the

load, is attractive, light and free-draining. A simple deck for a small roof is easily made, but any major works and all repairs to an unsound roof are best done by professionals. The cost of employing them will be less than that of repairing and putting to rights the results of water infiltration: rot, collapsing plaster, stained walls, ruined carpets and the rest.

Before going even this far, consult landlords or building superintendents and check on any local ordinances. There may be restrictive clauses in the lease regarding alterations or additions, while planning and building permission are sometimes needed, especially where alterations to the building's façade or profile will visible. Access to fire-ladders or communal walkways must be kept clear at all times. Neighbours may appeal successfully against a garden on a back-extension, seeing it as a threat to their privacy. Nevertheless, all such difficulties can usually be overcome with a little flexibility, so let us assume that the structural research is done, the necessary permissions are obtained and there is a sound, waterproof roof to work on.

Access is often a problem, not only for ourselves but for the installation of pots, plants, soil, furniture, ornaments and so on. Most are bulky and heavy; who is going to manoeuvre them up stairs or into lifts (elevators)? It is a good idea to measure the internal dimensions of the stairwell or the lift before rushing out to buy tall trees and gazebo kits; if they will not go in vertically, they can often be squeezed in diagonally.

While it is possible, at a price, to have everything hoisted up and delivered by a crane, most things (trellis, light containers and garden sundries) can be hauled aloft by an easily rigged-up pulley or pulled up by a rope; special pots and plants go up in baskets or plastic ground-sheets, the kind with a handle at each corner through which the ropes are threaded. A strong man can carry astonishing loads on his back up a ladder or fire-escape. Whenever possible use one of these methods; they save a lot of grief. If things must go through the house, some mess is inevitable, so cover the carpets, place all pictures, ornaments and fragile furniture well out of the way and watch out for the wall-paper.

Try to get the style and design of the garden established in the mind before dealing with the remaining practicalities: safety, unruly winds, excessive shade, fierce sun. On a roof we do not necessarily have to take the surroundings into account (very often there are none of significance) and the architecture of the house is probably irrelevant. The only limitations placed on the imagination are a possible lack of cash, the available space and the climate.

Trellis panels temper the winds but allow air to circulate. Except in the hottest zones, the heat of the sun is usually more blessing than hazard, for shade is not difficult to provide. In cooler areas the residual warmth from the walls and rising from the floors below is an asset. Rain settles the dust and freshens up the plants, but in summer is unlikely to penetrate the foliage in sufficient quantities; in winter, alas, it is apt to overdo things, battering the plants and waterlogging containers.

All rules of taste can be broken, for few but ourselves will be affected; if gnomes are loved, this is the spot for them, with scarlet toadstools and plastic ivy too. Or the mood might be classical, recalling ancient Greece and Rome: columns, broken pediments (fibreglass or timber) and shattered urns. Then again we might choose a taste of the Orient, a sunbather's paradise, or a child's

*Railway
sleepers edge
this raised
pool and seat*

*Railway
sleepers
make the
step to this
raised deck*

*Built-in
table and
seating with
storage space
beneath*

*A roof garden: timber
decking with built-in
storage seats and a table.*

Boulders

*Slightly lower
deck*

*One of two
pavilions
hidden in
planted areas*

playground. It would be pleasant to try something less familiar – a mini-jungle of palms, bananas and exotic climbers (vines), a minimum-upkeep, high-tech fantasy of scaffold poles, canvas awnings, gleaming metal and outrageous plants; a garden of faded canvas chairs, of sand, stones and drift-wood, planted with sea-thistles, thrift, and so on, somewhat in the style of that remarkable garden made by the late Derek Jarman, the brilliant film-maker. In hot, dry climates, a roof garden of cacti and succulents would be practical and interesting, though some sort of shaded seating-area would be most necessary. I would also like to try the kind of garden done so well by the American landscape architects Oehme and van Sweden, composed mainly of massed perennials and large sweeps or clumps of grasses in all their forms and colours, from the tall fountains of miscanthus to the low, hummocky things; even in autumn and winter there would be the seed-heads and the beautiful bleached colours.

The peripatetic might prefer a painted garden. Mirrors, trellis, murals, *trompe l'oeil,* all on removable panels, along with painted plywood cut-outs of trees, statues, pillars, urns, etc. All illusion, but, with folding table and chairs, artificial grass or chequerboard squares of decking all easily picked up, this is a lightweight garden for all seasons that could be moved and resurrected time and again. It would require neither watering nor weeding, although one might sneak in a pot or two of real flowers and some culinary herbs.

Many would be happier with something like the marble-paved roof garden high above Paris made for Marcel Boussac by Russell Page (who did not think much of roof gardens on the whole). He describes how, with more space at his disposal than most, it contained two small pavilions, one at each end, and, to hide the chimneys and link the pavilions, a covered gallery of trelliswork in the Chinese Chippendale manner, painted white and dark green. Wings of ivy-covered trellis at each side screened the neighbouring buildings and concentrated attention on the view of the Bois de Boulogne. Large planting boxes, also painted dark green and white, together with a few terracotta pots set along the parapet, were filled with tulips and pansies in the spring, followed by scarlet geraniums and white petunias in summer. The photographs show it to be an urbane garden, not too difficult to copy or adapt to a smaller scale.

Much less austere is a double roof garden high above the city where the owner has chosen to complement several artefacts from China and Thailand. The walls are sky-blue, covered by white trellis in the Chinese style. On each of the two flanking walls, the trellis has been shaped into an arch and the wall within painted 'Chinese red' as a backdrop for a marble head of the Buddha. At the outer corners of the terrace is a pair of small, purely ornamental pavilions in the same style, each containing a statue. All the plants are in dark blue glazed containers from Thailand. On the sunnier side, a silver olive tree has come through several winters and for the rest, there are mostly evergreen plants: the silvery, spiky astelia, rustling bamboos, pretty *Convolvulus cneorum* with its delicate white flowers, the aromatic cistus, neat hebes with stumpy spears of pink, purple, white and lavender flowers, the sword-like phormiums, glossy *Pittosporum tobira* with it scented cream flowers, rosemary, santolina, senecio (*Brachyglottis* 'Sunshine'), yucca, and other sun-lovers, underplanted with small-leaved ivies and white summer bedding. Honeysuckle, passion-flowers, trachelospermum (the variegated form, which takes on pink tones in winter) and fragrant *Jasminum humile* 'Revolutum' cover the trellis.

On the shadier side grows a strawberry tree, more bamboos, a variegated fatsia, choisyas, *Camellia* 'Lavinia Maggi', that chic camellia with red-and-white striped flowers, plus a vast specimen of the holly-like *Osmanthus heterophyllus* 'Gulftide', reliable *Viburnum tinus* and some rhododendrons, all underplanted with tobacco plants, busy-lizzies and fuchsias, while ivies, evergreen honeysuckles and x *Fatshedera lizei* clamber up the trellis. The iron railings are lined with toughened PVC for wind-protection and as a safety measure for visiting grandchildren, who are unable to get a foothold on the smooth surface. It is not in any way a Chinese or Thai garden, but one that has adopted various echoes of oriental styles and combined them, in a totally unembarrassed way, with whatever the owners liked or needed for their comfort. The result is pretty and laid-back, but this sort of relaxed mixture would only work happily on a roof garden, I think.

But back to the practicalities. First the water supply, absolutely essential here where both wind and sun have a desiccating effect; then the drainage, equally vital. Fit some kind of cover over the downspouts so that they do not become clogged with soil and plant debris; inspect and clean these regularly. Electricity makes the roof even more charming at night, with the usual combinations of up, down, side, back and front-lighting, of 'grazing' lights and strings of fairy-lights. If that is too ambitious, use oil-lamps or hurricane lamps on the table, or candle-lanterns and night-lights in glass jars.

Storage is tricky on all but the largest roofs. Where there is room, a decorative little hut can be used or the empty space beneath a built-in seat. Otherwise use a storage bench, barrel or pot, as described in the previous chapter.

The boundaries must be sound, secure and of a reasonable height, whether they be walls, fencing, railings, trellis or panels of toughened glass and plastic. Raise a low wall or parapet to a safer level by adding railings, balustrades or boxes (good when planting-space is limited), but fix these firmly.

The existing walls may give sufficient protection, but where the garden is surrounded by high buildings which act as wind funnels, something more may be needed. Once it is established from where the ill-winds blow, a screen of some sort can be erected on that side, perhaps by building a slightly higher wall. Trellis is excellent; it softens the wind, gives a degree of privacy and supports the plants, yet allows light through. Even where privacy is not a problem, there is something comforting about an area of lightly enclosed space which is particularly welcome beneath a vast sky. It has the same effect, in its way, as that of a blanket spread on the grass or on the beach; our territory is marked, and a 'palisade' is erected between us and the rest of the world. When a roof is large enough, make sheltering islands of greenery in planters or containers. These might swirl around the roof in a series of curving bays, one hiding a shady pavilion, another a pool or low reclining seat, while yet others conceal a statue or a dining-table and chairs.

Whenever there is a view worth preserving (and where there is, it is often spectacular), every effort should be made to do so. If, by ill-luck, it should be on the windy side, add glass or plastic panels here, or make some attractive moon-windows in the walls and screens. If, on the contrary, the view is the last thing you would wish to see, blot it out with thickly planted trellis and contrive a garden that keeps the attention within. Where privacy is desperately needed – or you find yourself eyeball to eyeball with complete strangers in an adjoining building – use close-set paling. Overlooked from a greater height? Frustrate Peeping Toms by erecting a pergola or an awning of some kind so that there is at least one safe area.

Paint or stain all softwoods; in shade, white, bright or warm colours are pleasant, but in the open use muted tones to reduce glare: black, greys, blue-greys and greenish-blues, aubergine, indigo, rose-madder and the dark, soft, moody greens.

If something more rugged is needed, rustic poles, rough planks or floorboards are useful and can be set vertically, horizontally or diagonally. High, vertical and close-set planks are good where there are children, being virtually impossible for them to climb. Split-bamboo screening makes a subtle backdrop for cane furniture, palms and other architectural evergreens, boulders, etc. Hurdles of willow, hazel, reed, brushwood, woven heather-screens and so on have a countrified feel. At the seaside, screens and awnings of canvas or manmade textiles such as Terram look suitably nautical. Whatever is chosen, fix it, and indeed everything else, very securely, for gales wreak havoc, and the danger of those below being struck by flying debris is very real; check your insurance.

Plants make an attractive and effective screen on any roof large and strong enough to take substantial planters: those worth trying include tough evergreens like spotted laurel, cotoneaster, elaeagnus, euonymus, holly, privet, yew, *Thuja plicata* 'Atrovirens' and *Viburnum tinus*. Bamboos are excellent while dogwood, hawthorn and hornbeam are among the deciduous plants that do well on a roof.

Floor surfaces, already touched on, will be very much a part of the design. There are lightweight roof-tiles available, usually in white, off-white or black, unobtrusive enough, but not exactly exciting. Tiles of toughened glass let light into the rooms below while making an attractive pattern of squares on the roof. Lightweight pavers, marble, terracotta, ceramic and quarry tiles are excellent and may be laid in all the ways described in the previous chapters. Stone slabs are only for the stoutest roof, but gravel can be used on any sound surface if there are efficient drain-covers.

Here is one of the few places where artificial grass is acceptable; easily cleaned with a hose and a stiff brush when necessary, marvellous for sunbathing and restful on the eye if a soft, olive-green is chosen. The real thing (perhaps using Grodan, a lightweight, inert substance that maintains plant-life), is only for masochists, I think, for who is going to mow it, and where is the mower to be kept?

Planks, old floorboards and decking are excellent; leave them in natural wood colour (treat softwoods with preservative) or use a stain from the wide range of shades; try black, which gives a sophisticated feel, is restful on the eyes and a good foil for plants; a mixture of pinks, mauves, purples and silver looks particularly well against black.

On the larger roof, decking and planks can be laid fore-and-aft, side-to-side, diagonally, in chevrons, or in combinations of any of these to give a directional pull to a design, to guide the eyes towards a view, or once again to hold the attention within the palisade.

Well-made trellis, the simplicity of the planting and, of course, the view, make the most of this small but stunning roof garden in New York. (DESIGNER Tim Du Val)

Walls are treated in the same way as those of a courtyard: paint, trellis, mirrors, murals, *trompe l'oeil*, false arches, etc., and given the same decorative objects: wall-masks, plaques, tiles, collages or whatever, for anything goes here, if we get it right. A sunny wall is a good place to fix up a little shade; blinds, awnings or some kind of simple, lightweight arbour or pergola, draped with plants. Incidentally, a roof is practically the only safe place for the rampageous Russian vine (*Fallopia bald-schuanica*), for here, grown in a container, its rapacity is easily controlled; although tough, its leaves and white flowers are delicately charming. Most climbers (vines) recommended in earlier chapters can be tried, if sheltered from the very worst of the elements.

Further planting depends on the available space. Purpose-built roof gardens often come with sizeable raised beds: if not, they are usually strong enough to take the weight of any you want. Because space here is so limited, chalk the outlines of proposed beds, pools, planters, containers, tables, chairs, ornaments and so on, on the roof, to make sure they will fit in with sufficient space for circulation round them.

Raised beds and planters can be built of bricks, rendered blocks, railway sleepers (cross-ties) and planks. The greatest care must be taken to see that no drains, downspouts or gullies are blocked. There is also the danger that faults and weaknesses may develop unseen beneath them; I prefer, therefore, to make them free-standing. The bigger the planters and containers, the less moisture is lost from the soil and the greater the protection for plant roots from excesses of heat and cold.

All the usual kinds of containers discussed in more detail in the following chapter can be used. Lightweight versions will reduce the strain on the roof and the backs of whoever has to lug them around. Such things as plastic and rubber storage tanks are useful, but not exactly stylish; disguise them with a screen of tongue-and-groove or painted plywood (exterior quality) and trellis. Plastic containers look tacky; paint them and perhaps add bands of another shade. Alternatively, sponge, drag or stipple several colours and shades of paint over one another to disguise the containers' plebeian origins. Such treatments also work for tin-cans and other light but humble containers. A galvanized water-tank makes a good-sized container; it should have a few drainage-holes drilled into the base. Paint to resemble an antique lead water-cistern in dull, dark grey, dragged with traces of matt-black paint, or black-lead (for fire grates, sold in a tube). Sponge with blue-green paint to imitate copper and verdigris.

On all but the most robust roofs, place the heavier containers round the edges, where the roof is strongest. To gain more floor space, place boxes and troughs on the parapet and include some ground-cover roses and other trailing things among the other plants to make a tapestry curtain. Where there is even less room, hang windowboxes on the outside of the walls, using special brackets; secure them further by bolting to the brackets or tying on with extra-strong galvanized wire.

It may be tempting to use hanging and wall-baskets on a roof garden, but this temptation is almost always to be resisted, for they are better suited to pubs, riverboats and municipal planting schemes. They need such frequent watering that unless you install an automatic system there will be little time for anything else in hot weather. Either they will shrivel and die or drip for hours on all and sundry.

Whatever beds, planters or containers are used, give them a good drainage layer (broken polystyrene foam is cheap and light) and consider the compost (soil mix) carefully. Apart from the special needs of individual plants, this should be light and reasonably free-draining to prevent waterlogging in the rainy months, yet it must be dense enough to give the plants a secure anchorage and to prevent moisture evaporating rapidly in hot weather. Lining containers with black plastic will help to prevent the latter; remember to make drainage-holes.

For most plants I like to use a loam-based compost (soil mix) and add varying amounts of coarse grit and vermiculite plus at least one-third of peat or a peat-substitute, depending on the type of plant. Plants that prefer a particularly free-draining soil, for instance, need a greater amount of grit and vermiculite, while there are lime-free mixes for those plants that need them. It is a good idea to top all containers with a light dressing of gravel to retain moisture, prevent soil splashes and protect the roots from cats.

A pool is all the more fun on a roof, perhaps because it seems such a ridiculous concept if one comes to think about it. If weight is a problem, one must be satisfied with a wall-fountain or a shallow dish to mirror the sky, one that doubles as a birdbath. Of necessity, a roof-pool will nearly always be a raised pool, and in most cases, a small one. Nevertheless, there should be room for at least one small waterlily, a couple of marginal plants, a floater or two and some underwater oxygenators. Most of the usual kinds of raised pool can be used, but again, they must go at the margins of all but the strongest roofs.

Fish should be happy enough as long as the pool is about eighteen inches (45cm) deep and you give them some extra shade (a tile or a length of drain-pipe balanced on a few bricks). An old water cistern, large bowl or barrel makes a good pool for a miniature waterlily and a couple of fish, but they should be brought in to the safety of a bowl or tank in winter, for such a small volume of water is likely to be frozen solid, unless there is a pool-heater. On the other hand, in areas of intense summer heat, the temperature of the water in a roof-pool might well be too much for the fish; there one must be content with aquatic plants alone.

On a grander scale, one might draw inspiration from a water garden designed by Sir Geoffrey Jellicoe, set high up on the roof of a department store and described as uniting earth and heaven. The roof was flooded to a depth of nine inches (23cm) between curvilinear islands of trees, plants and cobbles. Tall, curving screens of bamboo canes were placed around it to give shelter from the wind, while the circular stepping-stones appeared to float lightly across the surface of the water, which alternated as a ruffled sea and a mirror to the ever-changing patterns of sky and clouds. There seems no reason why something similar should not be done in a domestic setting, but again, this would need professional advice and expertise.

Small trees have great charm on a roof and give some useful shade if room can be found for them; exotics in hot regions look wonderful, while in cooler areas quite a few things that are on the borderline of hardiness are worth trying: azara, bay, mimosa (*Acacia dealbata*), eucalyptus, olive, pittosporum and so on are all delightful. Hardier, wind-tolerant varieties include birch, cotoneaster, crab-apples, dogwood, hawthorn, honey-locusts, rowans, sea buckthorn, tamarisk, privet, the silver-leaved willow (*Salix exigua* – particularly pretty and delicate-looking), a weeping Siberian pea (*Caragana arborescens* 'Walker'), and the silvery Russian olive (*Elaeagnus angustifolia*).

Given good drainage, most of the silver-leaved plants that like a Mediterranean climate do very well, while such things as oleanders and citrus trees are a possibility, although their survival cannot be guaranteed unless they can be taken inside in the cold months. Plants with an architectural interest are always effective on a roof. Thin conifers and spiky, sword-shaped things (astelia, cordyline, dracaena, phormium, yucca, and so on) contrast with bushy and spreading plants while bamboos, fatsias, figs and trailing vines, together with palms such as *Trachycarpus fortunei*, give a lush, tropical effect.

Fruit-trees, grape-vines, runner beans, courgettes (zucchini), herbs and saladings are worth a go where there is room, while tomatoes are a good bet. Even potatoes can be grown in a barrel and strawberries, not surprisingly, in a strawberry pot. All the usual annuals, for sun and shade, do just as well, if not better, on a roof and most bulbs will put on a good show, at least for a season or two; the smaller varieties and cultivars of all plants are less likely to be blown over by the winds.

Close-meshed trellis, a well-planted, rectangular wall-trough and the interesting table and chairs make this decked roof terrace in San Francisco unusually elegant. (DESIGNER Christian Wright)

'Sculpture can cause no end of grief,' Lanning Roper remarked, and the weight of any ornament must be considered, while those on or near the edges should be fixed very securely indeed, as it is only too easy to knock them over in a careless moment, with results that do not bear thinking of. There is an excellent range of fibreglass 'antiques' (ornaments, cisterns, pots, urns, olive-jars and so on) that are very light and extremely convincing; some of these are just as effective when left unplanted – and, of course, much lighter.

Never be deterred by lack of space, for the smallest roof garden I know, high above Bond Street in London, is only about six by eight feet (180 x 250cm) wide and long. Decking covers a domed roof-light, while the far wall and a small gate are trellised, so that the latter, although still functional, is almost unnoticeable. Small plants and containers might have been chosen, but instead an enormous fibreglass Ali-Baba jar squats in one corner and several large, evergreen plants with big leaves are grouped about in handsome pots, while others sprawl over the walls. Oddly, this tiny garden does not look overcrowded; rather it seems one has stumbled into a small, mysterious corner of a tropical garden.

Many balconies are even smaller than this, but, whatever their size, may be treated in many of the same ways as a roof garden, for they share much the same problems. On the smallest, privacy and protection from the winds may be hard to achieve, but many have the advantage of a roof which gives a little shade and shelter; it is fun to paint such a roof with a sky of sun and clouds, or moon and stars (something to admire when sunbathing). Where wild winds make planting difficult, why not also paint a garden on the back wall? If no permanent structural additions are allowed, we may get away with shelter provided by removable screens and roll-down blinds. In these tiny spaces, containers placed on or hung outside the parapets and walls are desirable and others will squat happily on shelves and wall brackets; just for once I would even countenance the occasional hanging basket. Fish and miniature water plants will thrive in a small bowl or windowbox. Any plants that climb up the walls or hang down from the containers need to be tough. Wind-tolerant plants for this sort of situation include honeysuckle, Russian vine, sweet peas, scarlet runner beans and ivy, but most annual climbers (vines) will do well if put out when the the worst of the winds are over; both trailing nasturtiums and ivy-leaved pelargoniums are excellent. All the little, flat wall-decorations are useful as well as hanging things – ornate bird cages, mobiles, wind-chimes and so on. Folding tables and chairs that double up for indoor use are invaluable here, oil-lamps (kerosene-lamps) are pretty at night and miraculous meals have been cooked on tiny Japanese-style barbecues. Roof gardens or balconies – all in all, the sky's the limit.

These roofs shrugging, relaxed, these sun-warmed bricks,
Smooth, rounded bays, they are like lovers in bed
At ease, knowing and known. Cats stalk here...

MARGARET STANLEY-WRENCH (1917–74)

9

CONTROLLED DISORDER AT THE HEART OF EVERYTHING

Containers

I like the habit of pot gardening. It reminds me of the South - Italy, Spain, Provence, where pots of carnations and zinnias are stood carelessly about, in a sunny courtyard or rising in tiers on the treads of an outside stair, dusty but oh how gay! I know it entails constant watering, but consider the convenience of being able to set down a smear of colour just where you need it.

VITA SACKVILLE-WEST (1892–1962)

OPPOSITE: *In summer, a small country terrace bursts with colour from containers filled with abutilon, agave, bidens, cordylines, yellow argyranthemum and many other plants, large and small. (The Old Rectory, Berkshire)*

*P*OT GARDENING – how infinitely more appealing that sounds than the dreary 'gardening in containers'. Pot gardening has an honourable history: we know from wall-paintings that the Egyptians grew many things this way. In Greece it is said to have been associated with the cult of Aphrodite, which spread rapidly across the ancient world and gave rise to the bizarre 'Adonis Gardens' – pots filled with soil at midsummer and sprinkled with seeds which, once sprouted, were allowed to wither and die (sadly reminiscent of much pot gardening today). Nevertheless, in time this miserable usage gave way to that of actually encouraging the plants to live, and we have never looked back.

Trees, shrubs, climbers (vines), roses, perennials, annuals and bulbs: there is a pot or tub of one kind or another to suit them all. The larger ones have permanent or semi-permanent positions here and there; smaller, lighter things can be moved around at will. This is useful anywhere, but invaluable for those who have little space; not for us the spring border, the summer border and the winter garden; we must cram all our seasons into the small amount of room available. The easiest way to do so is by changing the pots around as the months progress, bringing on extras from the wings for their brief, glorious moment at the heart of things, then banishing them backstage to recover their strength for another year or to wither and die tactfully out of sight. All this combined with the ability to place that 'smear of colour' just where and when it is wanted, yet without having to watch decaying foliage for weeks on end – one could ask for little more.

All of us have our failures: plants that wither or fade just when we need them most, others suffering accidental deaths at the hands of children and animals (and which of us, in an unguarded moment, has not stepped back upon some treasure or other?). This is bad enough in any garden, but

when everything is laid out beneath our noses in a small one, the loss is like a missing tooth in the mouth of a beloved. At such times a plant in a pot is invaluable, for it can be dropped into the empty space and replace the dear one while adding some useful height and a different accent at the same time.

This ability to add instant height around the garden is a particularly useful attribute of pot gardening; here in my small courtyard, several chimneypots, collected over the years, perform this service admirably. I never tire of finding different plants for them. Last year it was the graceful *Fuchsia magellanica* 'Versicolor', an excellent plant for a high container in light shade as its drooping delicacy can then be appreciated more fully.

Then again, a plant in a container often brings a sculptural element to the garden, a piece of topiary, for instance, or something of an architectural nature. One cordyline, standard bay or box (boxwood) spiral, in a pot that – like the crown of Mr Salteena in *The Young Visiters* – is small but costly, could be decoration enough for a little courtyard, while such frivolities as peacocks, hens, teddy-bears and tea-pots lighten everything up when there is a danger of the garden becoming too staid.

CONTAINER PLANTS

Most plants will grow in containers for some time, but those suggested here are particularly good and should be happy for considerable periods. Climate zones have not been given, as such artificial conditions make them unreliable. Plants that are tender in any area can often be grown if they are given extra protection or bought inside in cold weather.

TREES AND TREE-LIKE SHRUBS
Acer negundo and cvs.
Arbutus
Camellia
Caragana
Cordyline
Elaeagnus angustifolia
Eucalyptus
Fatsia
Ficus 'Brown Turkey'
Ilex (most),
Laurus nobilis
Malus
Prunus
Salix caprea 'Kilmarnock'
S. exigua
Also all topiary plants and dwarf
    conifers

SHRUBS
Abutilon
Acer palmatum cvs.

Artemisia
Aucuba
Brachyglottis 'Sunshine'
B. monroi
Buxus
Ceanothus
Choisya
Cistus
Convolvulus cneorum
Daphne
Dracaena
Elaeagnus
Euonymus
Fuchsia
Hebe
Helichrysum petiolarie
Hydrangea
Lavandula
Myrtus
Nandina domestica
Ozothamnus
Pittosporum
Rhapiolepis
Rhododendron – small species,
    hybrids and cvs.
Rosa (many medium to small roses
    do well, inc. climbers, shrubs,
    cluster, polyantha, patio, minia-
    tures and standards)
Rosmarinus
Salvia
Santolina
Skimmia
Teucrium fruticans

Viburnum
Vinca
Yucca

CLIMBERS
Clematis
Cobaea scandens
C. s. alba
C. althaeoides
C. tricolor 'Heavenly Blue'
Hedera
Jasminum
Lathyrus odoratus
Lonicera
Passiflora
Polygonum baldschuanicum
Rhodochiton atrosanguineus
Sollya
Thunbergia alata
Trachelospermum
Wisteria (needs a large container)

PERENNIALS
Agapanthus
Agave
Astelia
Bergenia
Brugmansia
Dicentra
Geranium
Glechoma hederacea 'Variegata'
Heuchera
Heucherella
Hosta

Iris
Ophiopogon
Phormium
Pulmonaria
Sedum
Sempervivum
Tolmiea
Zantedeschia

BULBS, CORMS, TUBERS
Small things usually do well for a
while and larger successful
subjects include daffodils, lilies,
tulips and hyacinths but these are
seldom so good in subsequent
years.

ALPINES
Most will thrive, given a gritty, well-
drained compost.

GRASSES, BAMBOOS, FERNS
Most grow very well in containers.

For some of us pots, troughs, windowboxes and other receptacles are all there may be by way of a garden, yet that has never hindered the enthusiast. The very limitations seem to be more spur than deterrent. A good 'pot garden', generously planted, brings controlled disorder to a fine art. With the aid of a container or two, gardens of sorts can be made on any tiny space we can find: pots of colour on each step cheer up the dreariest flight of concrete stairs; a couple of small tubs on either side of a porch have enough soil for a climbing rose and some honeysuckle, a couple of lavender bushes and half a dozen annuals to give us a warm welcome.

The tiniest 'garden' I ever made was at the back of a small town house that appeared to have no possible scope for even these small pleasures – not even a window-ledge or a doorstep. The main room, at the back of the house, overlooked some particularly unattractive lock-up garages. The owners of the house were desperate to block these out and to see a little greenery. We fixed an extra-large windowbox (supported on robust metal brackets) outside the one window and just level with its sill. This was planted with a climber (vine) at each side, low evergreens and tall annuals. Some way below this we made a strong, outsize ledge to accommodate a large trough, which took two more vigorous climbers and some tall and feathery evergreen shrubs. Then we made a high, three-sided trellis screen and this was fixed round the windows to screen out the garages and support the climbers. Soon, all that could be seen from inside the drawing-room was a delicate tracery of small flowers and greenery; barely a glimpse could be caught of the offending buildings. Just occasionally, if someone was a little careless with the watering-can, an agonized cry would float up from the mechanics below. This is a common hazard for neighbours of the container gardener, one we should try not to cause.

I must confess to being an avid collector of receptacles of all sorts, for really they have everything – charm and versatility, drama, elegance, mobility and romance, even humour. Most of us have our favourites, whether it be an inherited treasure, the generous present of a friend, or a holiday souvenir lugged home from some dusty wayside pottery. Setting out to buy, we are faced by a bewildering choice: the old, traditional tubs, flower pots, windowboxes and troughs have been joined by a host of others brought in from all over the world. Before succumbing to temptation, there are several things to be considered.

Containers may be of wood, metal, stone (and reconstituted stone), marble, slate, cement and concrete, clay, terracotta, glazed ceramics, fibreglass and plastic, all with their advantages and disadvantages. For practical reasons, anything that has to be moved frequently, or that is set on a balcony or roof, should be as light as possible. In parts of the world subject to winter frost, containers that can withstand it are desirable.

Apart from a few serendipitous finds, we usually 'gets what we pays for', and excellence has its price. Considering the impact that even one magnificent vase can have in a small garden, to choose the best one can afford is a worthwhile investment; unlike a fitted kitchen, a good container accompanies us from place to place, and is passed on to the children when we return to the soil.

That said, it is worth keeping the mind and eyes open: almost anything capable of holding soil can be used as a receptacle if a few holes are drilled in the base so that excess water drains away. I once planted a garden for a darling man who insisted that we used his collection of ammunition boxes, and have to admit that when painted and covered by trailing plants they looked not at all bad.

Then there is the familiar problem of the chicken and the egg: do we buy the pot for the plant or the plant for the pot? Most of us do a bit of both, I suspect: we fall in love with either a delicious pot or some totally irresistible plant, then desperately search out a compatible partner for them, to say nothing of a suitable place for them to sit. To adapt an old adage, there should be a pot for everything and everything in its pot.

In a garden, as within a house, objects of real excellence can be used in a wide range of periods and settings, but there will always be some pull between the architecture or period of the house and the largest, most prominently positioned containers. In the rarefied garden of a period house, classical iron vases, terracotta urns and carved stone baskets look suitably distinguished, but even here there will always be some corner for humbler things and a little wit; no garden should be taken too seriously all the time.

Almost anything with rural or domestic origins, including the kitchen sink, looks natural in a cottage garden: painted tyres, chimneypots, tin baths, milkchurns, buckets, pots and pans, kettles and so on, as well as the simpler versions of all the more conventional containers. I would be chary of installing yet another wheelbarrow planted up with violent annuals, but perhaps if one came across it full of ancient flower-pots, ivy, nettles, or with a miniature wildflower lawn, it might be redeemed.

Much the same applies to a seaside garden, but here a salty note creeps in: an ancient dinghy sinks beneath a flood of nasturtiums, conch-shells spout ferns beside the back door and a parrot's cage hosts a trailing geranium or some house-plant hung out for a summer airing.

In general, the plainer bowls, pots, troughs and vases of stone or clay fit happily into almost any design. Fibreglass containers are ideal for roofs and balconies but now come in so wide a range of styles that they are useful in many other places, for apart from being light, they are easily cleaned, need little other maintenance and retain moisture for longer than clay or timber. Square tubs or *caisses* of the Versailles type, together with the rather similar rectangular troughs and windowboxes, are especially urbane, while 'lead' water-cisterns and 'clay' oil-jars are admirable in a romantic garden or courtyard.

Any container set against the bold lines of contemporary architecture needs to be equally striking if it is to make a worthwhile contribution. Here one can use serious timber planters, the largest concrete pots and troughs and the more sculptural shapes of terracotta, filling them with plants of equal distinction. Potters working in the modern idiom may have something particularly suitable for this kind of garden, but I cannot resist quoting A.D.B Wood again: ever the pragmatist, he remarks of a large concrete container that 'its real advantage is that its height renders it safe from the salutations of all but the tallest dogs'. He has a point there and if you have a dog this should be borne in mind. I speak as one who has lost countless treasured plants in this way, and now measures any prospective pots against the dog's vital parts to ensure that the plants at least will be out of range.

Often, places and plants cry out for a particular container, and *vice versa*; it is a game that can

In this narrow garden, containers of many different styles have been used to grow a variety of exotic-looking foliage plants, including box boxwood, maple, hosta, brugmansia, cypress, cordyline and a treefern. (DESIGNER J. Bailey)

be played for hours, moving a plant from pot to pot, and the pot from one position to another, until at last both insist that this is it, the right and only choice.

Think of a large oil-jar, which never looks better than when some delicate trailing thing cascades down its sides: a small-flowered clematis (*macropetala* or *alpina*, for instance), or the trailing ground-ivy, *Glechoma hederacea* 'Variegata'; even the little ivy-leaved toadflax, *Cymbalaria muralis*. Such jars are particularly effective if set upon a raised base, such as a low square of bricks or stone placed, say, at the centre of a rose garden or the meeting of four paths.

Vita Sackville-West described how they planted the great Chinese jar at Sissinghurst, by first surrounding it with blue oxypetalum and plumbago, then dropping a pot of the morning-glory 'Heavenly Blue' into the top and allowing it to pour down the jar's aubergine sides, in, as she said, a symphony of different blues; a similar symphony could be played in many a smaller garden and in other colours.

Then there are the true *caisses de Versailles,* set on either side of a door, or lined out along a terrace, very much on their dignity, haughtily demanding bay trees, citrus trees or some other handsome evergreen lollipops.

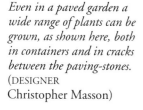

Even in a paved garden a wide range of plants can be grown, as shown here, both in containers and in cracks between the paving-stones. (DESIGNER Christopher Masson)

On the other hand, the familiar wooden half-barrels, banded with metal hoops, are so honest and unpretentious that they can be used in virtually any garden, large or small, grand or humble. They are the best possible home for multicoloured polyanthus in spring, for massed tulips and forget-me-nots and for an old-fashioned hydrangea, setting off its oval leaves and great mop-heads to perfection.

Spiky plants, the agaves, yuccas and so on, seem to look their best when jutting from an almost spherical pot or one that somewhat resemble an egg-cup. A round-shaped plant looks neat when set in a square container or in a traditional flower pot.

Often we use a plant in a container of some kind, either singly or with a twin, as exclamation marks, or visual 'clues', drawing attention to the edge of a terrace, a change of levels, the corners of a pool, a flight of steps, an arch or a gateway. We might place another as a full-stop, something for the eye to rest on at the end of a path or vista. Frequently, we emphasize them in some way, perhaps positioning them on a pedestal or on a small, raised plinth, on the piers of a wall (overflowing with petunias, pelargoniums and *Helichrysum petiolare*), and framed by an alcove or trellised arch. If such an arch is mirror-backed, the plant will seem to be partially screening another part of the garden beyond.

I use a large cordyline in this fashion, placed in front of a mirror-backed arch on a south-facing wall; it is planted in a clay jar that we found in the early fifties, lying neglected behind an old black barn in the grounds of our first house. It is of the wide-mouthed, rounded shape with a pronounced rim and a *cartouche* at each side, often associated with Gertrude Jekyll. As we were not far from Munstead, where she lived, I like to think it could have been given by her to the previous owner, a dedicated gardener, much of an age, who might well have been an acquaintance. The fact that a giant cow parsley (*Heracleum mantegazzianum*), something of a favourite of Jekyll's, grew beside the barn seems to increase the likelihood of this. Whatever its history, it is one of my most prized possessions and, despite its weight, has accompanied me to every subsequent garden. Some forty years on, by happy accident, I found an identical pot (but one size smaller) in a near-by junk shop. It is rapidly becoming equally indispensable and at the moment sits happily in a corner of dappled shade, accommodating a little maple that has finely dissected leaves.

In another, shady, town garden, a disused doorway is blocked off for security reasons. The slight recess that remains is painted lemon-yellow and houses a well-planted vase, full of variegated ivies and white annuals, on a pedestal. The yellow background sets off the plants and provides a high note among the surrounding and rather sombre greens, so that it makes a satisfying termination to the design.

Paving details set off a strategically placed container. At the centre of a square of flagstones, for instance, there might be a circle of tiles or slates set on edge and infilled by cobbles or random paving, with perhaps an old copper boiler (kettle) at its heart. I like to put the lovely glaucous-leaved hosta, *H. sieboldiana* var. *elegans*, in these coppers, the whole shape sculptural and the colours in perfect accord. Soft pink pelargoniums also look delicious there, but for high drama, a mass of scarlet tulips is sensational.

Or again, in either gravel or grass, a square made by railway sleepers (cross-ties) or a circle of granite setts will set off a tub or a stone trough. In much the same way, a small clipped hedge, round or square, makes a neat frame for a large pot, perhaps one surrounded by low-growing annuals or frothy alchemilla.

As to colour, the more gaily we plant, the more restrained should be the container. Anything brightly patterned would offer too much competition to the flowers, so that *faience* and similar ceramics are best kept for foliage plants or clipped evergreens, in the way that the garden designer Anthony Noel places small box (boxwood) spheres in his jolly striped flower pots. A fatsia or a green Japanese maple of spreading habit is just the note for an egg-cup-shaped jar that swirls with dragons or improbable flowers.

Pots containing standard trees of hard and soft fruit can be set in the middle of a small bed or group of lower pots, while the familiar strawberry-pot makes a charming centrepiece for a herb garden.

Then I like to have little groups and clutters of pots, large or small, dotted around in odd corners of the garden and up flights of steps (one cannot afford to waste space in a small garden), filling them with lilies, more and more lilies, and with mini-collections of plants: foliage of contrasting shapes and textures, herbs, scented-leaved pelargoniums (very much at home in old flower pots) and some low-growing alpines, sedums and sempervivums, happily overflowing their shallow clay seed-pans, and so on.

One of the joys of gardening in this way is that no matter what the garden soil, one can grow all sorts of odds and ends that demand special conditions. Some, such as herbs and alpines, grown in old sinks and troughs, like a gritty, free-draining soil, while more greedy feeders grow fat in a rich, moist mixture of loam, well-rotted manure, leafmould, peat and garden compost. A lime-free mix enables us to grow small rhododendrons, azaleas, camellias and the like.

A row of trees, large shrubs or tall bamboos in troughs or long planters is particularly useful for screens and boundaries when the garden floor is solid. They also give instant height to a scheme and make secret corners to frame a seat, a pool or an ornament. In my tiny garden, a large pot contains a variegated fatsia, a tall fountain of miscanthus and a trailing fuchsia; these hide a small bench both from the house and the neighbouring upstairs windows, suggesting a *giardino segreto* on the smallest scale.

The evergreen magnolias do well in large containers, though in cooler countries they may then be shy to flower; I have been told by a nurseryman that the variety 'Galissonière' is the most likely to oblige. Such handsome creatures deserve equally handsome containers, a *caisse de Versailles* or hand-thrown terracotta pots.

Camellias, too, need a dignified holder and for once, a tub will not really do. Try a *caisse* or a *Vaso da Camelia*. Oh, those Italian pots – *Vaso Festonato, Vaso Normale, Orcio da Anfora Liscio, Orcio da Giardino, Jardinière Decorata* – they sound like something absolutely delicious from the menu of an upmarket trattoria and one would like to have them all.

Sadly, valuable plants, together with their equally precious containers, are at risk, particularly

in a front garden, and should be secured in some way. Concrete and clay pots may be cemented in (as long as the drainage holes are not obstructed), and wooden tubs be secured by heavy chains which also go round the plants. Neither of these measures gives complete protection, but they buy time and will deter the casual villain.

Where there is a conservatory, a sun-room, even a glazed porch or frost-proof shed, all kinds of tender plants may be overwintered there and brought out in summer to stun the beholder: citrus, abutilon, oleander, stunning blue plumbago, *Melianthus major* with its glaucous, goffered leaves, agave, agapanthus, beautiful, deadly brugmansia or indeed anything that is not normally hardy in our gardens, wherever they may be. Standard plants of tender anisodontea, fuchsias, marguerites, etc., bring welcome height and colour to many parts of the summer garden, fuchsias being especially useful for shady corners. On a smaller scale, I am very fond of the silver-leaved, pink-flowered *Convolvulus althaeoides*, and although here it survives (so far) in the sunniest corner, in many places it would need to be coddled in winter.

If it is not possible to bring in pots and tubs, they may be given winter overcoats of bubble-plastic (it looks better if covered with sacking) or horticultural fleece (spun-polyester or Reemay) which can be further padded out with bracken, straw or leaves; this also helps to prevent the roots from freezing.

When it comes to the smaller things – perennials, annuals, and bulbs, either used as under-planting to larger subjects, or on their own – there are two approaches, the restrained and the voluptuous. In the first, just one plant or a mass of the same variety is used; in the second, a riotous assembly of mixed plants jostles for attention, overflowing their pots with joyful exuberance.

An unfettered mind and open-handed generosity, even profligacy, are the keys to success with mixed planting. In windowboxes especially, unless going in for the sort of chic understatement that uses two spheres and a central cone of clipped box (boxwood), only some really prolific planting works; anything less looks mean-spirited and faintly depressing. As to hanging baskets, avoid them like the plague, but if you insist, let them be as blowzy as cancan dancers, all frills, thrills and unbuttoned bounce. I do not wish to encourage their use, but if you must, they are easier to plant if you place the basket in a bucket or pot to hold them steady while you work.

Apart from using the best of the long-familiar plant associations in a container, one should never be afraid to experiment. There are colours that blend softly with each other and others that, *concordia discors*, spark off the rest; both mixtures are delightful in the right place. We can place one

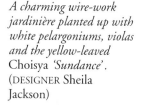

A charming wire-work jardinière planted up with white pelargoniums, violas and the yellow-leaved Choisya *'Sundance'.* (DESIGNER Sheila Jackson)

plant against another and stand back to see what they do for each other, then add something else or perhaps several other things, and maybe remove a few, repeating this until satisfied. Tuck a few wild-flowers (grown from seed, not taken from the countryside) into the containers from time to time or drop in some house-plants here and there.

There is also the profile of a plant or a group of them to consider. Apart from the bizarre outlines of bonsai, and the neatly sculpted shapes of topiary, one can use the upright conifers, the thrusting sword-blades of a phormium, a fountaining grass, or some low, hummocky festucas. There are the neat little mounds formed by hebes such as *Hebe topiaria* and 'Pewter Dome', as well as plants that will grow in a loosely horizontal fashion – *Ceanothus thyrsiflorus repens*, prostrate junipers, *Begonia rex* and so on.

Many groups of mixed annuals in pots and vases benefit from the central height given by astelias, cordylines or dracaenas. In winter, containers filled with plants that have polished bark and coloured stems, gnarled or twisted branches, berries, catkins and seed-heads all have a special part to play, a striking one when caught by the dying sun or glittering with frost. When there is no room to grow such things, one can always cheat a little, buying them in from florists to stick into existing pots.

Slim, pliant twigs, such as those of willow or hazel, make little domed cages over a pot, both to support and protect the plants and as a winter decoration in their own right; two or more stems are bent over and each end is pressed well down into the soil, then the centre may be tied with a little bass or garden twine. Further stems may be woven in and out around the bottom of the dome, basket-fashion.

Whatever the plant, the pot and the compost (soil mix), there are a few basic rules for filling up a container. First, see that it is absolutely clean, washed and scrubbed. Next, to prevent soil being washed out, cut a piece of horticultural fleece (Reemay) to size and line the bottom of the container (J Cloths are a good substitute). Then place crocks over the drainage-holes, followed when there is room by a further layer of drainage material, which might be stones, coarse gravel, fired-clay granules; the depth of the layer will depend on the size of the pot, but between one or two inches (2.5–5cm) is usually about right for all but the smallest, with another inch or two added to the very largest containers. In these, where the plants are like to stay for several years, I like to add a layer of old turves, chopped up and set grass-side down, followed by some well-rotted manure before topping up with compost (soil mix). Smaller plants that can be repotted every two or three years can do without this and besides, there is unlikely to be room for it in their pots.

Once the plants are in place and have been watered and firmed in, mulch with gravel, stones or chipped bark; this stops birds and cats from chucking the soil about, keeps moisture in and excesses of heat or cold out. There should be enough space left at the top of the pot so that it does not overflow when watered.

On the vexed subject of watering, never go solely by the weather, for often rain will not get through the foliage, while pots in the lee of a wall may get little or none at all. Nor is the surface of the soil to be relied on; I like the time-honoured test of sticking a finger right into the soil to see how things are down below. If moist, leave well alone, but when dry, a good soaking is called for, which is much better than a regular but half-hearted sprinkle.

In hot sun or drying winds, it may be necessary to water containers once or even twice a day; early morning and the evenings are the best time for this, but it is better to water at any time, rather than not at all. If there is an automatic watering-system, check regularly to make sure that it is not supplying too much or too little.

Because water must be given so often, nutrients are leached out; to redress this, regular feeding at weekly intervals is advisable during the growing season. I prefer a liquid feed, using a tomato fertilizer for the flowering plants, and whatever is appropriate for anything with special needs. If the garden is likely to be left for long periods, water-retentive polymers and slow-release fertilizers can be added to the compost (soil mix) at planting time.

As to aftercare, regular dead-heading of the flowers and the removal of any dead wood or dead, diseased and yellowing leaves helps to keep things healthy and long-flowering. Spraying to prevent or treat pests and diseases may be done by those who do not disapprove of it; there are some sprays which do both jobs and also contain a useful foliar feed.

One problem is increasingly common and not all that easy to deal with. Vine weevils are

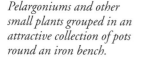

Pelargoniums and other small plants grouped in an attractive collection of pots round an iron bench.

appearing in many gardens now and containers seem to be particularly susceptible. Mine have suffered badly; I had to change all the compost (soil mixes) last year, a tedious and expensive process. Leaf damage is one of the first signs in spring and summer, as the adult beetle hides during the day and emerges at night to munch its way round the edges of the lower leaves. The revolting little grubs – plump, white and shaped like croissants – stay below ground and chomp through the plants' roots from autumn until spring, so that the first one knows about it is when some cherished plant collapses and dies without warning. There is not all that much to be done except for regular inspections, scrupulous hygiene with the containers and the prompt removal of all debris from around the garden. Biological control seems to offer some hope, but I have not yet tried this.

Where pollution is a problem, it may be necessary to wash the leaves of evergreens occasionally; a job to be done on a mild day when there is time to spare. Perched on a stool, with a bucket of slightly soapy water to hand, it is as pleasantly relaxing a way to spend an hour or so as any other.

'If neither pond nor tanks are available, waterlilies, like Diogenes, will content themselves with a tub, and find themselves quite at home in half a cask, buried in the ground and filled with soil and water,' wrote the old French plantsman Maurice Vilmorin, and in the smallest gardens a very satisfactory little pool can be made in a tub, trough or pot, which, having been emptied, may be taken with us when we move. Anything that holds water will do, but with metal, which may be toxic to fish, give the insides a coat of rubber paint.

With these small pools, one can have a fountain, or plants and fish, but not all three, for the latter will not be happy with the turbulence caused by the former in such a small space; a fountain may be placed in either sun or shade. Some plants will tolerate a shaded pool, but fish and waterlilies need sun for at least the greater part of the day; any container for them should be as large as possible, something between eighteen and thirty inches (45–75cm) wide, and as deep as possible. Even so, as said before, the fish will have to be taken to an inside tank in winter or moved to a larger pool if one is available. Pool, plants and fish could overwinter happily enough in a conservatory, but watch out for any pensive cats that might be about.

With a couple of fish, one or two of the dwarf waterlilies, maybe a few marginals and a submerged oxygenator, the container pool will be a charming thing. Two or three such pools are even better – unless, that is, you agree with Francis Bacon (and I hope you do not) that 'Pools mar all, and make the garden unwholesome and full of flies and frogs.'

> *Forward, to where in borders, pots and tubs*
> *Stand sturdy and delicious Trees and Shrubs!*
> *Well-dressed Camellias flourish with the Bay,*
> *Which is as stately, not so bright as they.*

RUTH PITTER (1897–1992)

~ 10 ~

Apropos of Garden Statuary, Sir

Ornament and Decoration

A little garden, if too simply treated, soon exhausts our curiosity. The more the designer lacks space the apter should he be in making us forget our garden's limitations. Ingenious pleasantries of treatment here and there arrest the interest. By concentrating it they make the visitor oblivious of the smallness of the theatre which yields so much diversion. Ornament of the right kind is even more welcome in small gardens than big, but needs to be used sparingly.

GERTRUDE JEKYLL (1843–1932)

OPPOSITE: *A delicate metal obelisk highlights this leafy corner and brings it into focus.* (DESIGNER David Ffrench)

BUT WHAT SHOULD WE INCLUDE under the heading of 'ornament of the right kind'? I take it to cover any decorative thing, even if it has a use. All those ornaments described here, large or small, might just as well be used in other gardens, but carry that much more weight in a small garden: their positioning will be more crucial, their style, texture and colour have a more profound influence.

Furniture, for instance, may be the most important decorative element in a tiny courtyard: a chair or small bench could well be the only ornament. Every garden needs at least a table and one or two chairs, even if the latter must be folding café-chairs: simple, adaptable, with enough *éclat* to be a decorative part of the whole. With a little more room, a good-looking bench of some sort can be added.

The style of these things will depend upon personal taste and the ambience of the garden, but it is seldom wrong to take the simpler of two choices. Again, it pays to rifle through books and magazines to see just what might give a lift to a particular garden and how the colours and shades of the various paints and stains play a part.

But to start with the garden gate. A front garden should have a decent gate, for nothing sets it off so well. Fine ironwork is traditional for period houses and some old cottages, but a timber gate can also be a handsome or even, occasionally, a delicate, latticed thing: it pays to match the gate to the house. Similar houses near by may still have their original iron or woodwork; this is expensive but rewarding. Keep a camera handy to snap likely specimens. Piers and finials are important, while the garden railings must be considered. Antique shops and dealers in architectural salvage often have

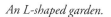

An L-shaped garden.

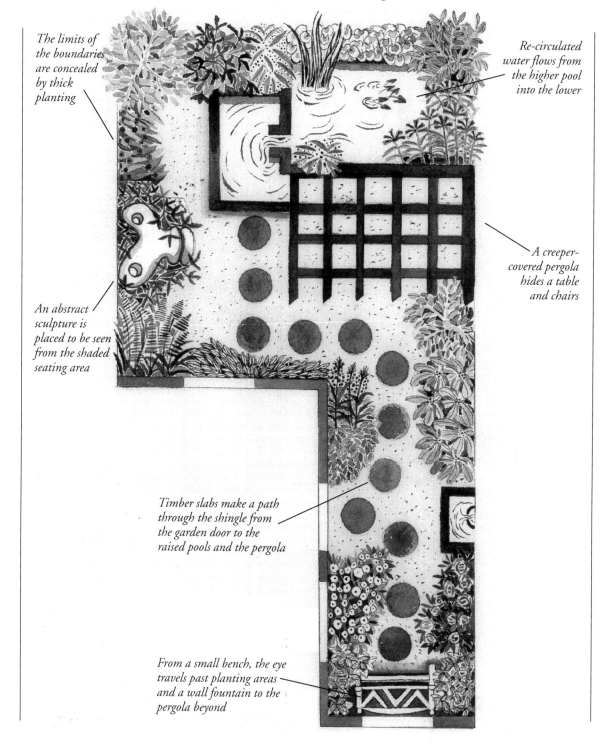

The limits of the boundaries are concealed by thick planting

Re-circulated water flows from the higher pool into the lower

A creeper-covered pergola hides a table and chairs

An abstract sculpture is placed to be seen from the shaded seating area

Timber slabs make a path through the shingle from the garden door to the raised pools and the pergola

From a small bench, the eye travels past planting areas and a wall fountain to the pergola beyond

suitable gates, railings, porches, balconies and other such decorative things.

By their vertical nature walls provide much space-saving scope for ornamentation that is useful in small gardens as it allows the centre to be kept free. There may be existing alcoves, recesses, unusual doors, windows and decorative brickwork details. An arch or doorway (real or false) in a wall intrigues, inviting us on. Brick roundels fitted with mirror-glass become small 'moon-windows' or *oeils de boeuf;* as with mirror-backed arches, these give an illusion of space while bringing more light into the garden. When new walls are built or old ones repaired, similar features can be incorporated as work progresses and may be given further emphasis by paint or by a frame of plants about them. An alcove, for instance, or a recess formed by a blocked-up window, when painted in contrast with the surrounding walls (perhaps a dark blue recess in a pale blue wall, or *vice versa*) makes an excellent background for a statue or an urn. Or paint a simple arch-shape on a wall, fit it with a decorative bracket and perch your urn or marble bust there; a miniature version of this would enhance even the tiniest garden. Ivy or some other evergreen climber trained about it, or in a circle around a window, plaque or wall-clock, makes a neat, emphatic frame.

Walls play host to all sorts of other decorative things: murals, masks, ceramic tiles and platters, panels of bas-relief, collages, sundials, dovecotes, wall-fountains and so on. Here on the far wall I have two 'mandalas' – simmering-plates from an iron range discovered when opening up a chimney-breast. Coal-hole covers of the last century, which are often very decorative, could be used in a similar way. Gaudi, the Spanish architect, used coloured fragments of broken tiles to decorate a wall; the same technique can be used for a plaque or panel, perhaps incorporating any shards that turn up when the garden is dug over. I like to use things found in this way (jars, horseshoes, ancient keys, bottles), for it gives a pleasing sense of continuity. Collages may be of metal, timber, paint,

An unusual small garden, full of arresting ornamental effects. The mirrored arches on the deep blue wall, the mosaic of the pool echoing the same shades, the black spiral in the pebble paving and the two primitive heads all play important parts in this striking design. (DESIGNER Ann Frith)

One end of a small and shaded basement area, painted a warm shade of terracotta, has been arched over to form an alcove for an outsize antique statue. (Mrs Caroline Walker's garden: DESIGNER *Angela Kirby)*

ARCHITECTURAL PLANTS

Topiary and mop-headed standards have sculptural qualities while many trees and shrubs become architectural with age.	*Ficus* Z7 *Magnolia* (evergreen) Z7 *Rhus* Z3	x *Fatshedera lizei* Z7 *Hedera*, large-leaved spp. to Z6 *Vitis*, esp. *V. coignetiae*, Z5	*Euphorbia characias* Z7 Ferns (many) esp. *Matteuccia struthiopteris* Grasses (many)
	SHRUBS		*Gunnera*, to Z7
TREES AND TREE-LIKE SHRUBS	*Acer palmatum* Z5	**PERENNIALS**	*Helleborus argutifolius* Z7
Acer japonicum Z5	*Choisya* Z7	*Acanthus* Z6	*Iris*
Aralia elata Z4	*Fatsia japonica* Z8	*Agave* Z9	*Kniphofia* Z8
Catalpa Z5	*F. j.* 'Variegata'	*Angelica archangelica* Z4	*Ligularia*, to Z4
Cordyline Z8	*Mahonia*, to Z6	*Astelia* Z9	*Onopordum*, to Z6
Cornus alternifolia Z3	*Yucca*, to Z4	*Bergenia*, to Z3	*Phormium* Z8
Dracaena Z7		*Crambe* Z6	*Rheum* Z6
Eriobotrya japonica Z7	**CLIMBERS**	*Cynara* Z6	*Rodgersia*, to Z5
Eucalyptus Z8	*Clematis armandii*	*Echinops*, to Z3	*Sisyrinchium* Z8
		Eryngium, to Z6	

driftwood, sea-shells and whatever else comes to hand. If one cannot afford to buy, and the design of them does not come easily, abstract paintings provide inspiration; there is no shame in such borrowings.

Enhance any low walls in the garden with a stone coping or a balustrade where this would not look pretentious. Use spheres, pineapples, urns, vases as finials, or try something more curious: a pile of flints, large fossils and shells, a sheep's skull. Walls and trellis go together as love and marriage used to do; again, being vertical, it is a natural choice for a small garden, used to form patterns and illusions on a wall – flat arches, alcoves, columns, pediments and so on. The lattice may be square or diamond-shaped, wide-meshed or close-set. Combinations of these will define and emphasize the design. For instance, a run of square trellis topped by a narrow, diamond-shaped band, or the other way round. A trellis screen finished in this fashion, placed at the edge of the paved area, wall to wall, with a couple of arched openings giving access to the rest of the garden, makes a sheltered dining-room.

Out in the garden, obelisks of trellis make superb supports for roses and other climbers but they also have a sculptural quality; a series of them, used directionally, has a unifying effect as we follow them down the garden. Two or three hoops or flat arches, either of metal or cut from plywood, can be used in the same way.

Water is the finest of garden ornaments: pools, canals, rills and so on all make their contribution to the mood. A well-head of carved stone is a traditional centrepiece for a courtyard or formal garden; more simple affairs of brick or local stone are fine for a cottage, as long as there is not the slightest hint of kitsch. Troughs or raised pools are excellent space-savers, fed from a spout or wall-mask from a shell or a jar or some character at the pool's edge. A long, narrow trough against a wall, water splashing into it from a row of spouts above, takes up little room and is charming in a small garden. Container-pools are perfect for a tiny courtyard or a roof garden, but birdbaths are aesthetically dodgy and I prefer to use a shallow dish of some kind or a giant clam shell.

Fountains, wall-mounted or free-standing, range from the classical to the contemporary by way of the bizarre. There are some good contemporary designs, but consider commissioning a young sculptor to make one for a particular garden; this could be far more interesting than most things available commercially. On a larger scale, the British designer John Stefanidis has bordered the cobbled floor of an enclosed, rectangular garden with a narrow canal of shallow water. A bronze frog squats in one corner and a bench is placed between the clipped embrasures at each end. Although this is part of a large country garden, something similar would be just as satisfying in the city; the maintenance would be minimal.

Garden buildings are excellent focusing devices. Even a shed can be an ornament if trimmed up, painted and strewn with climbers; a narrow little thing about the size and shape of a sentry-box will fit virtually anywhere, including roof gardens and basement areas. Give it finials and other trimmings, a coat a two of grey-blue paint, then smother it with vines and roses and it becomes the main attraction of a small garden: take off the door and it houses a small chair, a statue or an urn.

Grottoes are engaging curiosities. In a shaded place they would seem a natural choice, with ferns, shells, stalactites and a little mossy pool at the heart of all, water trickling over the green stones. The remains of a brick shed, outside privy – even an air-raid shelter (where they still exist) – might give one the beginnings of the thing, while the angle of two walls would be another place to try. I see it as hidden away at the end of a path of shingle and crushed shells, beset by trailing ivies and other bosky evergreens. It could provide a home for all the holiday shells and accumulated junk-shop buys of minerals, crystals, fossils, corals, etc. River gods, naiads or a bronze frog would be at home there; with luck, real toads and frogs will arrive.

Summer-houses and gazebos, bowers, arbours, tunnels and pergolas all have their charms and uses. Tunnels make pleasantly shaded walkways which mark the transition from one part of the garden to another while framing some object at the farther end; a seat, statue or urn, for example. Try them also in the shape of a cross at the centre of the garden. They are very beautiful when dripping with roses, yellow and purple racemes of laburnum and wisteria, or fruiting vines ... as one William Horman noted in about 1519: 'A vyne clevynge to hys railes with hys twyndynge stringis and lette hangynge downe hys clusters of grapis, maketh a pleasaunt walkyng alleye.'

Pergolas are rather more solid: wooden cross-beams are laid across two parallel beams, supported by rows of stout, upright timbers or metal poles. Easy enough to make, but anyone who is up to a little bricklaying might try a pergola with piers of brick or stone.

For the rest of us, there are plenty of such things to be bought and dozens of styles to choose from. A wirework pavilion is very light, and therefore particularly useful for a roof terrace. There are similar porches and some flat wirework panels with an arch at the centre. Fixed to a wall, these make excellent frames for a statue or a raised vase. A pair of such porches would provide the underlying support for a green garden-house, in the style of the sweet-bay pavilion at the Villa Noailles, where

PLANTS FOR TOPIARY			
Buxus microphylla and cvs. (box, boxwood) Z6	Hedera helix (ivy) and cvs. (good for 'false' topiary) Z5	Laurus nobilis (bay) Z8	buckthorn Z7
B. sempervirens and cvs. Z5	Ilex aquifolium (English holly) Z5	Ligustrum (privet) Z7	Taxus (yew) Z6
Crataegus (hawthorn), to Z5	I. crenata (Japanese holly) Z6	Lonicera nitida Z7	(Other evergreens can be trained
		Rhamnus alaternus (Italian	as mop-headed standards)

evergreens are trained and clipped up and over the wire framework until it is completely covered: ivy, rhamnus or privet are suitable smotherers, quick-growing and resilient.

I think of an arbour as a free-standing structure, and probably domed, while a bower I see as a sort of deep arch with its back to the wall – but perhaps it is the other way round? Several suppliers offer both bowers and arbours in either timber or metal, with and without built-in seats, and these should take only an hour or two at most to put up. Again, a blacksmith would make up an original design.

An excellent retreat for a very small garden is easily made by putting one or two beams or scaffold-poles across the angle of two walls. Once these are covered with a climber (vine) or two, it has as much charm as many a more fanciful affair. Make a little more of it by raising up the ground by a step or two, and giving it a floor of tiles, stone, bricks or cobbles – in fact, of anything that will be in contrast to the surrounding surfaces. Age the beams a little by flogging them with a length of chain: brutal but effective on all wood that is too new and perfect (the brave can also try this on new stonework). Planks supported on bricks make a seat for it, but one or two chairs, or maybe a very small bench, could be used instead.

Where a central position against a wall or fence is desirable, the quickest solution is to use either the wirework porch already described or a wide, deepish garden arch (available from garden centres, by mail-order or homemade). Three or four trellis panels also make a very easy bower; two panels for the sides, and a shorter one for the top. Narrow lengths of timber are used to make the

In a very small garden, a decorative bench may be all the ornament needed, or indeed possible, but here there is also enough room for a hedgehog to snuffle his way along the edge of the raised pool. (DESIGNER Thomasina Tarling)

frame and a fourth panel might be fixed across the back to strengthen it further before the whole thing is secured to the wall; finials or a little pediment cut from plywood can be added as embellishments.

In one of those long, narrow strips, so often found behind a town house, the garden has been divided into three sections, running between raised beds at either side. First comes a paved area in front of the French windows, for a table and chairs, then two wide, shallow steps lead down to the central area of herringbone brickwork, which has a rose bed at the middle. Another flight of steps at the far end leads up to a semicircle of random stone paving where there is a statue in a white-trellised pavilion. It is all very simple and charming; anyone could make such a garden in a few days. Both the central rose bed and the pavilion pull the eye away from a brutal block of flats beyond and down into the garden. Elsewhere, the pavilion might be replaced by a small pergola and the central rose bed could just as easily be a lily-pool.

A temple, however small, lends distinction: it need be only the suggestion of one, a couple of pillars and a pediment. The manufacturers of reconstituted stone supply everything needed, including flagstones for the temple floor. If everything is chipped or knocked about a bit and toned down with a few coats of diluted liquid manure, it quickly acquires an antique look. But take care, all the pieces are horrendously heavy; they can crush or amputate fingers and toes that get in the way. Lighter versions of timber or fibreglass are safer and would be essential on a roof. Something on the same lines, but with a tiled or slate roof instead of the pediment, much in the style of a loggia, may be built all along the back wall of a garden or courtyard – an excellent place to sit, and a fine termination to a design.

Similar but lightweight temples and porticoes can be made of plywood, and painted or stained: black or dark green, for instance. The first would look well with black-and-white paving-squares and the latter, perhaps, with gravel. A good example of this type of thing was a restrained and reflective town garden designed in the eighties by three British sculptors, Carter, Fulcher and Tate, which used plywood, trellis, mirrors, gravel, topiary and gilded spheres to great effect. It is just this sort of artifice that can work so well in an urban terrace.

Apropos of spheres – since a child, I have always been fascinated by those gleaming glass 'witch's balls', but would not have thought to use them outside until recently when I saw two photographed in widely differing gardens. One was set on a tripod at the centre of a herb garden in Holland, while the other was placed on a low vase among a huddle of small, pot-grown plants in a gloriously cluttered San Diego garden. Both looked utterly right, a lesson to me on the importance of keeping an open mind and an appraising eye. A gilded sphere could be used in much the same way. I have a mind to smarten up a ball-cock with a little gold paint and try it out somewhere in my garden; or perhaps three, like a pawnbroker's sign.

Apart from temples and porticoes, columns can be used throughout the garden for their purely ornamental qualities and associations. One pillar carries enough classical baggage to transform the mood of a small garden; the fact that it is out of scale merely adds to its potency. Unadorned, a pillar is a striking architectural statement; draped with ivy, it becomes melancholic. An encircling rose turns it into just another romantic old softy.

In the same way, odd pieces of broken stonework and damaged statuary evoke varied emotional responses: fragments of a Gothic window, the ancient gravestone of a family pet, a truncated urn spilling ivy or nettles ... all conjure up a different mood or half-forgotten dreams. My

---

GRASSES & BAMBOOS

Carex morrowii 'Fisher's Form' Z8
C. oshimensis 'Evergold' Z7
C. elata 'Aurea', (Bowles' golden sedge) Z7
Cortaderia selloana 'Pumila' (pampas grass) Z5
C. s. selloana 'Silver Comet'
Fargesia murieliae (umbrella bamboo) Z5
F. nitida (fountain bamboo) Z5
Festuca glauca (blue fescue) Z5
Glyceria maxima variegata Z5
Hakonechloa macra 'Aureola' Z5
Helictotrichon sempervirens (blue oat grass) Z4
Luzula nivea (snowy woodrush) Z6
Milium effusum 'Aureum' (Bowles' golden grass) Z5

Miscanthus sinensis 'Gracillimus' Z6
M.s. 'Graziella' Z5
M.s. 'Variegatus' Z5
M.s. 'Morning Light' Z5
Pennisetum setaceum Z9
Phalaris arundinacea var. 'Picta' (gardener's garters) Z4
Pleioblastus auricomus (yellow bamboo) Z7
P. var. pumilus Z6
P. variegatus Z7
Sasa veitchii (bamboo) Z7
S. calamagrostis (silver spike grass) Z7
S. gigantea (feather grass, golden oats) Z8

PAVING PLANTS

FOR SHADE
Ajuga reptans cvs. Z4
Arenaria balearica Z6
Campanula portenschlagiana Z5
C. poscharskyana Z4
Lysimachia nummularia 'Aurea' Z4
Mentha requienii Z6
Soleirolia soleirolii Z9

FOR SUN
Acaena caesiiglauca Z7
Arabis Z6
Armeria maritima Z3
Aethionema 'Warley Rose' Z7
A. armenum Z7
Aubrieta Z7
Aurinia saxatilis Z7

Campanula portenschlagiana Z5
C. poscharskyana Z4
Chamaemelum Z3
Dianthus deltoides Z3
Geranium sanguineum Z4
Hypericum coris Z9
Lobularia maritima Z7
Lithodora diffusa 'Heavenly Blue' Z9
Lysimachia nummularia 'Aurea' Z4
Phlox douglasii Z7
Phlox subulata cvs. Z4
Sagina subulata 'Aurea' Z5
Thymus serpyllum cvs. Z4
Trifolium repens 'Purpurascens' Z7
Veronica prostrata cvs. Z6
Sedum (low-growing) Z4

nineteenth-century nymph has lost both her feet and her forearms but none of her demure charm; the amputations hardly matter and in any case are mostly hidden by the surrounding plants.

In another tiny city garden a pair of marble hands, clutching beakers, are placed one at either side of a shaded step that leads up to the small lawn. Chipped, cracked, and only about nine inches (23cm) high, they froth over with white impatiens, conjuring up parasols, a frou-frou of long skirts on the terrace and the thin sound of a distant piano. In quite a different mood, we might use other broken fragments: a head or a hand rising from a small pool, a pair of feet diving in to another or a limbless torso afloat on a sea of greenery.

The more usual employment of statuary was neatly summed up by the English landscaper Thomas Mawson at the turn of the century; his words have just as much relevance today: 'Statuary may be of great use to the garden designer, assisting him to emphasize certain points in a way scarcely possible without it. This class of decoration has, however, been so much abused by the introduction of vulgar plaster or cement casts, and by figures manufactured in the tombstone-maker's yard, that it may be as well to state at once that it should be good of its kind or else omitted altogether.' He would not have approved of my nymph, for he added that 'marble and other cold and glaring materials are seldom in keeping with an English garden. Small lead figures and bronzes are much more sober and harmonious.'

While agreeing with Mawson in principle, there is nothing glaring about my nymph; over the years, moss and algae have turned her a sober and delicate green. I have found that these, helped on by a smear of yoghurt or a coat of liquid manure, have redeemed many a 'vulgar cement cast'. The better ones, treated thus and embraced by ivy or surrounded by greenery, are pretty good substitutes for the real thing in the dim light of shady town gardens.

Apart from marble, lead and bronze, statues are made of stone (and its imitators), concrete, clay, terracotta, fibreglass, wood, glass and glazed pottery. A small garden can be designed round whatever is chosen, using, say terracotta tiles, pots and so on to set off a matching statue. As Jekyll noted, 'The right placing of statues and vases is of as much importance as their intrinsic worth.' Attention is focused on just one statue, or a collection of them is placed around the garden, building up into a satisfying, kaleidoscopic whole. There are two main approaches, the bold and the subtle. In the first, a statue is placed in a position of some prominence; perhaps centrally, on the far wall, or set before a curving backdrop of evergreen, and probably enhanced in some of the ways already described – raised up, placed within an arch, etc. In the second approach, statues are discovered as if by chance, half-concealed by roses or ivy, lurking among a clump of bamboos, peering through a curtain of vine tendrils and so on.

Most of us could be more adventurous. Rather than choosing pale evocations of the past, we should be encouraging young sculptors, and even the not-so-young, for they go bravely on, practising an art that, like poetry, is often undervalued. Art galleries, local exhibitions and degree shows put on by art colleges are the places to look for interesting examples. Prices at the top are, rightly, quite steep, yet there are many good things that cost no more than dinner for two at an expensive restaurant, and just think how much longer the satisfaction will last.

A blue-glass witch's ball and a handful of glass marbles gleam amongst the green foliage of this small decked garden.

It is best to get one's eye in before buying, feasting on the best for a while, rather than rushing out to buy, on a whim, some expensive bronze girl or youth, often no better than coy tat or soft porn. If in doubt, stick to the abstract; a good abstract sculpture will be perfectly at ease even in a formal garden.

There are shops that import pots, statuary and various other artefacts from all over the world, many of which look wonderfully exotic. Travellers can bring such things back for themselves, even more satisfying and continues a long-established tradition. Pots and other receptacles for plants have been described in the previous chapter. Unplanted, many of them – amphora and pithoi, for example – because of their sculptural, evocative nature, can be treated as ornaments in their own right these are some of the most satisfying things to use in a garden. I know a romantic corner in a Polish artist's overgrown garden where an oriental coffeepot some three feet (1m) high, rescued from an abandoned café, enjoys retirement, its curves now delicately greened by verdigris.

Many 'found' objects stand in for statuary and reduce the strain on the budget: driftwood, gnarled roots and branches of old trees, skulls, boulders, stones and fossils all have sculptural quali-ties that contribute to the mood of the garden. They fit well into odd corners or, as with any orna-ment, can be given prominence, again by some emphasis in the surrounding paving and planting, or raised on a plinth of some kind, singly or grouped together as a still life. A sculptural plant (topiary, bonsai or architectural), can also be regarded as statuary, placed and used in a similar fashion,

A distinctive urn such as this is even more striking when strategically placed and left evocatively unplanted. (Peter Aldington, Turn End)

whether in a pot or in the ground. Thomas Church, in the garden of his Victorian house in San Francisco, clipped some mature evergreens in the Japanese 'cloud' fashion; the resulting plump little cushions of greenery seeming to float about in the air like a delightful mobile.

The smaller stones, shells, fossils and so on go anywhere, on windowsills and steps, grouped on a table, at the edge of a pool, apparently fallen by chance at the foot of a tree, or lying abandoned and half-submerged among ground cover. A topiary hen sits on a clutch of pebble eggs, a bronze snake slithers across the paving or a cluster of convoluted roots hangs like a bull's head over an archway. The line between originality and kitsch is a fine one, however; such things should not be overdone. 'If it be a high commendation to a writer or painter, that he knows when to leave off, it is not less so to an improver,' wrote the discerning Uvedale Price, an eighteenth-century Herefordshire squire much concerned with gardens and landscaping.

Then there are those garden accoutrements formerly for use but now largely decorative – weather-vanes, dovecotes, birdbaths, sundials, armillary spheres, etc. An old weather-cock looks charming, but I would hesitate to introduce a modern one; there are so many whimsical horrors about that one is quite put off most modern examples.

Occasionally a town dovecote is inhabited, but often they are merely for effect. I have quite a soft spot for them, in the right place (which, apart from those that are wall-mounted, is as far away from the house as is possible in a small garden); when the cote is inhabited, the amount of dung a few fantails can produce is frightening, if useful. There are other bird-houses about, some very ornate, even surreal, many of which are charming; what the birds think of them is anyone's guess.

As to sundials, I like these wall-mounted: it makes sense in a small garden where too much clutter at the centre unsettles things. If there must be an ornament there I would prefer a pool or a pot of some kind, but that is pure prejudice and if anyone pines for a sundial, they would be better off with something unusual from an artist-craftsman. An armillary sphere is an altogether superior thing: there is something about those rings, composed yet endlessly questing, that never fails to intrigue. Then, the last of this bunch, remember that those metal or wickerwork frames designed for the training of topiary, the birds, bears, cones, spirals and all the rest of the motley crew, make amusing ornaments when left bare.

In the gardens of terraced cottages all sort of odds and ends with domestic, horticultural or agricultural origins can spend a happy and loosely ornamental retirement: ridge-tiles and finials, tin baths, pots, pans, kettles, jugs, milkchurns, ploughs, lawn rollers, mangles (wringers), mangers, old implements, and the rest. Collections of jars, bottles, chimneypots and forcing-pots also look at home in small country gardens. Seaside cottages have shells, of course, and little piles of steamer glass, coiled chains, piles of cork and glass floats, lobsterpots, old sails, nets, ships' bells, toy boats, lanterns, oars, lengths of elaborately knotted rope and goodness knows what else. A ship's figurehead or an ancient anchor would be splendid, but are hard to come by. Incidentally, old wooden boats, set sharp-end up, make useful and ornamental seats. In industrial areas it is sometime possible to pick up pieces of mechanical detritus, and these look exactly right there: pulleys, cogs, wheels and giant springs, along with many other less easily recognized objects.

It is good to develop the habit of looking around with an appraising eye, but in the end, as Russell Page pointed out, 'A garden artist should only use decoration to heighten the style, that is the idea from which his whole construction has sprung. If he incorporates decorative adjuncts and accessory details, however picturesque, which are not directly related to his scheme, he will run the risk of diminishing the creative quality he should be seeking.'

There, then, that's done: with the last beauty-spot placed discreetly on the chin of the garden, as it were, there is nothing left for us to do but lie back in a comfortable chair and admire the fruits of all our hard work.

> *On thy bosom though many a kiss be,*
> > *There are none such as knew it of old,*
> *Was it Alciphron or Arisbe,*
> > *Male ringlets or feminine gold,*
> *That thy lips met with under the statue,*
> > *Whence a look shot out after thieves,*
> *From the eyes of the garden-god at you,*
> > *Across the fig-leaves?*

ALGERNON SWINBURNE (1837–1909)

BIBLIOGRAPHY

Anthony Archer-Wills, *The Water Gardener*, Frances Lincoln, 1993

John Brookes, *Room Outside*, Thames & Hudson, 1968
John Brookes, *The New Small Garden Book*, Dorling Kindersley, 1989
John Brookes' Garden Design Book, Dorling Kindersley, 1991

Thomas Church, *Gardens are for People*, Reinhold Publishing Corporation, 1955 (USA)

A.M. Cleveley, *The Integrated Garden*, Barrie & Jenkins, 1988

Marion Cran, *Garden Wisdom*, Herbert Jenkins, 1940s

Sylvia Crowe, *Garden Design*, Country Life, 1958

Mrs C.W. Earle, *Pot-Pourri from a Surrey Garden*, Smith Elder, 1898

Xenia Field, *Town and Roof Gardens*, Collins 1967

Good Ideas for your Garden, Reader's Digest, 1995
and all their other gardening books

Miles Hadfield, *Topiary and Ornamental Hedges*, Adam and Charles Black, 1971

Dr D.G. Hessayon, *The Rock and Water Garden Expert*, Expert Books, 1993

Gertrude Jekyll, *A Gardener's Testament*, Country Life, 1937
(and everything else written by her)

Geoffrey and Susan Jellicoe, *Modern Private Gardens*, Abelard Schumann, 1969

Jim Keeling, *The Terracotta Gardener*, Headline, 1993
Jack Kramer, *Your City Garden*, Scribners, 1972 (USA)
Jack Kramer, *Gardening in Small Spaces*, HP Books, 1979 (USA)

Christopher Lloyd, *Shrubs and Trees for Small Gardens*, Pan, 1965
Christopher Lloyd, *The Well-Tempered Gardener*, Collins, 1970
Christopher Lloyd, *Foliage Plants*, Collins, 1973
Christopher Lloyd, *Clematis*, Collins, 1977
(and everything else written by him)

C.E. Lucas Phillips, *Roses for Small Gardens*, Pan, 1965
C.E. Lucas Phillips, *The New Small Garden*, Collins, 1979

Peter McHoy, *The Garden Floor*, Headline, 1989

Michael Millar, *Making the Most of Town and City Gardens*, Treasure Books, 1985

Beverley Nichols, *Down the Garden Path*, Jonathan Cape, 1932

Russell Page, *The Education of a Gardener*, Collins, 1962

Pearson, Preston, Elliott, Waite, *Terrace and Courtyard Gardens*, RHS with Cassell, 1993

Vita Sackville-West, *In Your Garden Again*, Michael Joseph, 1955

Michael Spens, *The Complete Landscape Designs and Gardens of Sir Geoffrey Jellicoe*, Thames and Hudson, 1994

Violet Stevenson, *Patio, Rooftop and Balcony Gardens*, Collingridge, 1967

The Sunset Lawns and Ground Covers Book, Lane Publishing Co., 1979 (USA)

Thomasina Tarling, *The Container Garden*, RHS with Conran Octopus, 1993

Graham Stuart Thomas, *Shrub Roses of Today*, Phoenix House, 1962
Graham Stuart Thomas, *Old Shrub Roses*, Phoenix House, 1965
Graham Stuart Thomas, *Climbing Roses, Old and New*, Phoenix House, 1965
Graham Stuart Thomas, *The Art of Planting*, Dent, 1984
(and everything else written by him)

A.D.B. Wood, *Terrace and Courtyard Gardens for Modern Homes*, Collingridge, 1965

Linda Yang, *The City Garden Handbook*, Random House, 1990 (USA)

RHS Wisley Handbooks:

13. *Climbing and Wall Plants*, George Preston
17. *Hedges and Screens*, F.W. Shepperd
25. *Plants for Shade*, F.P. Knight
36. *Trees for Small Gardens*, Frank Knight

RHS Encyclopedia of Plants and Flowers, Dorling Kindersley, 1992
RHS Encyclopedia of Gardening, Dorling Kindersley, 1992

Index

ACKNOWLEDGEMENTS
The publishers wish to thank the following for permission to reproduce their photographs (identified by page number):

Eric Crichton 1, 21, 27, 29 top, 32, 39 l, 40, 47 top + btm, 50, 52, 55 r, 62 top, 85, 97, 99 l + r, 102 l, 105, 115 l, 135, 148, 151 l + r, 155, 156; Jerry Harpur 9, 15, 20 r, 39 r, 41, 49, 55 l, 71 r, 79, 116, 125, 136; Clive Nichols 11 top + btm, 12, 20 l, 23, 29 btm, 35 l, 62 btm, 67 btm, 70, 71 l, 72, 75, 77, 80, 87, 94, 102 r, 109, 115 r, ‡19, 128, 131, 139, 140, 147; Michael Nicholson 88; Steve Robson 2, 24. 35r, 38, 43, 57, 93, 142, 145, 152

Every reasonable effort has been made to trace copyright owners. The publishers would be happy to rectify any omissions in future editions of this book.

The quotation from 'Roof Garden', from *Selected Poems* by James Schuyler, is reproduced by permission of Farrar, Straus & Giroux Inc (Copyright © 1993 by the estate of James Schuyler) and Carcanet Press Ltd; the quotation from 'Other People's Glasshouses', by Ruth Pitter is from *Collected Poems* (Enitharmon Press 1996); the quotation from 'In the Winter', from *Villa L Allegria* by Osbert Sitwell, is reproduced by permission of David Higham Associates Ltd. The quotation from 'Hinterland' by Margaret Stanley-Wrench (reprinted in *The Oxford Book of Garden Verse*) is reproduced by permission of the estate of Margaret Stanley-Wrench.